Ismail Merchant's
FLORENCE

For Jim and Ruth

Ismail Merchant's
FLORENCE

FILMING AND FEASTING IN TUSCANY

ISMAIL MERCHANT

PHOTOGRAPHS BY DERRICK SANTINI

∾

HARRY N. ABRAMS, INC., PUBLISHERS

$\mathcal{T}$he traveller who has gone
to Italy to study the tactile
values of Giotto, or the
corruption of the Papacy may
return remembering nothing
but the blue sky and the men
and women who live under it.

E. M. Forster
A Room with a View, Chapter II

Editor: Mark Greenberg
Recipe editor: Ruth Peltason
Designer: Dana Sloan

All photographs are by Derrick Santini, with the exception of
those taken by Sarah Quill on the following pages: 2–3, 6, 14, 21,
24, 25, 28, 32–33, 36, 37, 40, 41, 44, 48 both, 50, 51, 78, 83, 89,
96, 98, 110, 111.

LIBRARY OF CONGRESS CATALOGING-IN-PUBLICATION DATA

Merchant, Ismail.
Ismail Merchant's Florence: filming and feasting
in Tuscany, 70 recipes / Ismail Merchant
p.   cm.
ISBN 0–8109–3639–9
1. Room with a view (Motion picture)
2. Florence (Italy)—Description and travel.
3. Cookery, Italian—Tuscan style.
PN1997.R575653M47   1994
791.43'72—dc20   93-36471

Printed and bound in Japan

On the title page: The Tuscan countryside

CONTENTS

~

INTRODUCTION

$\mathcal{M}$Y PARTNERS, James Ivory and Ruth Prawer Jhabvala, and I have been fortunate, given the diversity of our backgrounds and temperaments, to find so many projects that we all like and can work on as a team. But over the past thirty years of our collaboration we have just as often and just as passionately disagreed with each other on prospective ideas for films. Jim initially wanted to make *A Room with a View* partly because it was set in Italy, and partly for its story, which was more comic than our recent films and offered him new opportunities as a director.

From a writer's perspective, Ruth saw E. M. Forster's *Howards End* as his most complex and challenging novel and suggested we try and make that. I, on the other hand, felt that *A Room with a View* was the more accessible work and took an option on it. But the debate on the relative merits of the two books was academic because Jim suddenly didn't want to direct either of them. He liked both novels very much, but he wanted to do something different—a contemporary movie. We had no contemporary movie ready, however—no book or script ready to show to financiers or actors—while we did have a screenplay of *A Room with a View,* which Ruth had undertaken on the strength of development money from the National Film Finance Corporation (now British Screen).

So, Jim was persuaded, and I set about my task of raising money while we planned the film for May 1985. People ask me how I can plan to shoot a film when I have no financing. My answer to that is, plan the film anyway, set the start date, attract some actors, and the money will come, on the snowball effect.

From a production point of view it emerged that *A Room with a View* was a more practical prospect than *Howards End.* Though it would necessitate at least a month of filming in Florence, both logistically and financially it was the more reasonable of the two. Even so, it would cost approximately $3 million to make—more than we had ever before spent on a film.

Our first recce in Florence in February 1985 was inauspicious. I flew from Bombay to Rome and continued to Florence by rail. This long and tiring journey was made worse by a terrible bout of flu: I was running a fever, my head throbbed, my eyes streamed, my bones ached. The city wasn't in much better shape either, experiencing one of the coldest and wettest winters on record. Still, everything else was overshadowed by the enormous excitement of coming to Florence, a city I had never visited before.

Jim was already in Florence and came to meet me at the station together with Peter Marangoni, a friend from New York whose family lives in Florence, and who later became the associate producer on the film. Peter hauled me out of the train, clapped his arms about me, shouted, kissed me, ordered the porters around, tipped, met friends who then met me, and swept our party out of the station.

Being with friends in this overwhelmingly beautiful city was something to be celebrated around a dinner table. Unable to eat for days because of the flu, I suddenly had an appetite again—perhaps generated by the aroma of coffee in the station's espresso bars, or perhaps by my first sight of the markets just outside.

My introduction to Florentine cuisine came that night at a restaurant called Coco Lezzone, and with a first dish of tagliarini tossed in a sauce of olive oil, garlic, coriander, and black pepper, followed by an osso buco. I had eaten Italian food all over the world, including Italy, but nothing in the past could compare with this.

I thought perhaps I had discovered a great chef since, finally, it had been nothing more than a simple meal of pasta and beef: so the secret must be in the cooking. But Peter, a Florentine born and bred, told me that this standard of cooking was quite normal in Florence. He knew, of course, of my great passion for food and tantalizingly promised that I would eat in Florence as I had never eaten before. He said that of all the discoveries I was about to make in this city, the one that would most appeal to me was that Florence isn't only about art and history but also about life and good living: and here food, its preparation, and particularly, the enjoyment of it, amid the ambience of the dinner table and the café, played a principal part. Dinner at Coco Lezzone that night was, as far as I was concerned, a kind of tantalizing trailer for the big show that was to come.

Italians are born knowing the way. It would seem that the whole earth lay before them, not as a map, but as a chessboard, whereon they continually behold the changing pieces as well as the squares. Anyone can find places, but the finding of people is a gift from God.

E. M. Forster,
A Room with a View, Chapter VI

Ismail Merchant's
FLORENCE

*W*E STAYED AT the Pensione Quisisana on the recommendation of Peter's mother, Elizabeth Marangoni. As I had allowed only four days for this recce, she considered that the pensione's central location would be convenient and save us a lot of time.

The Quisisana overlooks the Arno at Lungarno Archibusieri, and a plaque on the wall, only inches below the lofty ceiling of the entrance, marks the level the Arno reached in the great flood of 1966. Two paces from the front door of the pensione and you are at the embankment of the river; three paces and you are *in* it. A few paces to the right take you to the Ponte Vecchio, and a dozen steps in any direction lead toward all the important landmarks of the city. It is well sited for everything—except floods.

Originally, because of Jim's passion for authenticity, we thought it might be appropriate to try and locate the site of Forster's original Pensione Bertolini and use that place for the film and also, perhaps, as our base. We were aware, of course, that this quest had eluded far worthier Forster scholars than ourselves, and finally, it also defeated us. It was not so much that we couldn't find the Bertolini, but that we found so many.

Years after writing *A Room with a View*, Forster recorded that on a later visit to Florence he had tried to locate his Bertolini, or the model for it, without success. His pensione had melted into several others, though there was no dispute *where* it had been: on the Lungarno, with a view of the hills on the opposite side of the river, and crowning one of these, the Romanesque church of San Miniato. This was the twenty-four-year-old Forster's view, just as it was Lucy Honeychurch's. But, as we were about to discover, it could not be ours.

We also needed a base for our production office, and it seemed that we had to look no further than the Quisisana. It was clean, comfortable, and convenient and, being of the right period, also a possibility as a stand-in for the Bertolini.

The Pensione Quisisana

I had made up my mind to appropriate the hotel and thought it fair to let the management know. I arranged to meet with Senora Marasco, whose family owns it, and who was responsible for running it. She was a very warm, intelligent, and practical woman who, I felt, would be able to cope with all the bizarre demands of filmmaking and filmmakers.

Senora Marasco said she would be happy to let us use the hotel, but she needed to know, not unreasonably, what dates we had in mind. Although we were committed to making the film, nothing had yet been finalized, least of all specific dates. She advised me that, in so small a city, hotel rooms were at a premium and heavily booked all through the year; and that if I needed a large number, it would be essential to book them immediately. She, herself, could offer me nothing beyond June. I made a quick calculation and decided. "Three months from now," I said. "Book us for the first week of May for one month." For May she had only sixteen rooms available, and that would be nowhere near enough to accommodate all the cast and crew and so on. There was really no time at all for hesitation as I knew that those rooms, too, would probably go soon. So I confirmed the reservations and asked for any cancellations as well. Then I tore out of the Quisisana and bolted through Florence booking hotel rooms. Four at the Excelsior, one of the grandest hotels in the whole of Italy, and that would do for our stars and director; two at the Rigatti; two at the Bristol—and on I went for the whole day booking every room I could find in the city for the month of May—the month when every tourist expects to be in Florence, the month when everything—the weather, the music, the spring flowers, and the spring delicacies are at their very best.

$\mathcal{F}$LORENCE IS A PARADISE for artists and historians and gourmets, but as I was about to discover, for a filmmaker it can be trouble. I tried to think of the films that had been shot in Florence but couldn't come up with any—it should have been a warning. We discovered that only two films had been made there: Minguzzi's *Melo*, and a film by Rossellini, called *Paisan*.

One of the key locations for the film was the Piazza Signoria where a murder takes place that causes Lucy Honeychurch to swoon into George Emerson's arms. From the Quisisana a short walk along the stately Piazzale degli Uffizi brings you directly and dramatically into the magnificent space of the Piazza. This Piazza is not only Florence's main tourist attraction but also a public thoroughfare, and even in early February it was far too crowded for my liking. We were told to take in all the details of the Piazza carefully for, by May, it would be so crowded that we wouldn't be able to see it.

The church and piazza of Santa Croce, other essential locations for the film, were no better. The thirteenth-century frescoes of Santa Croce and particularly those by Giotto in the Peruzzi and Bardi chapels are a magnet to art lovers all year round. That this is also the burial place of Michelangelo and Galileo only compounds the attraction. Above all, Santa Croce is still a functioning place of devotion and worship. So we could always expect to find it thronged.

Even more troubling than the potential hazards of the two main locations was the growing realization that, picturesque as the narrow streets and alleys were, they actually served as the arteries of the city. These cobbled medieval lanes were not the most efficient conduits of traffic at the best of times; and where a carelessly parked car can bring the city to a standstill, what the quantity and dimensions of movie-making trucks could do was mind boggling.

For all that, I was still enormously excited by the idea of making this film, and the one thing I never doubted was that in this city, where every view beckons provocatively for a camera and film crew, we would find not only the perfect view from Lucy's window (which we did not yet have) but could successfully re-create all the rest of Forster's Florence. Perhaps, however, I should have paid more heed to the first pages of the novel in which Lucy Honeychurch and Charlotte Bartlett, her cousin and chaperone, lament that they have been given a room with no view.

We, too, faced the same disappointment. We had no view. We scoured both banks of the Arno from top to bottom. We saw the wrong views, we saw views of television aerials and modern window shutters, of rush-hour traffic, views of almost everything except the essential one—the Arno with the church of San Miniato on its hill in the distance. So we shared Lucy and Charlotte's fate—except that they had been more fortunate. Alas, we had no kindly Emersons to offer us the view we wanted, and in time we had, in effect, to build one.

We could not look, as Forster had, across the Arno from the approximate spot (and height) of his vanished pensione. To the right were the somewhat ugly replacements of the old buildings blown up by the retreating Germans in 1944 (the commanding general, on a whim, spared the Ponte Vecchio, which leads there).

Fiesole with Florence in the distance

Opposite: The Piazza Signoria

15

On the left was a new traffic artery flowing downstream, like the Arno adjoining it, full of rushing cars. This was our dilemma, as we began shooting: where to find our view.

A KEY LOCATION we needed to find was for the picnic scene: a country lane for the carriage drive, an expanse of landscape for the picnic itself, and the little violet-studded valley where Lucy Honeychurch, through the sly intervention of the Italian coachman, stumbles accidentally on George Emerson—to be swept into his arms and kissed in the manner that Charlotte Bartlett found so alarming.

Our search for the country locations began in Fiesole, set high in the hills above the city yet only a twenty-minute drive from its center. The view from there was unimaginably beautiful and, even in winter, it was easy to see how this panorama of hills and slender cypress trees inspired Forster, generations of sensitive tourists and trekkers like him, and far back, Alessio Baldovinetti.

On the way to Fiesole Peter Marangoni suggested we stop for lunch at Le Cave di Maiano, a restaurant just outside the village of Maiano, near Fiesole. The building seemed so much a part of the scenery that it was as if it had just grown out of the hillside. In the summer, Peter told us, the tables are put outside in the garden and guests dine under a canopy of vines surrounded by lofty cypresses. The restaurant has been here for five hundred years, and for the last two hundred years it has belonged to the family of Aldo Landi, the present proprietor. Originally it was just a bottega catering to the miners from the nearby quarries of Monte Ceceri where they mined the famous *pietra serena*, the favored gray stone of Florentine sculptors and architects through the ages. And it was from Monte Ceceri that Leonardo da Vinci first attempted to fly.

Signore Landi greeted us, and recited the menu like a litany. His voice resonated around the old building, and I could almost imagine he was singing opera. Peter hadn't been exaggerating about Florentine food: the standard of Coco Lezzone was evidently the rule rather than the exception. Here we had another memorable meal—a fine fettucine, veal in a fragrant lemon sauce, and a dessert of spiced apples in a feather-light pastry.

I was completely baffled by the mystery of Tuscan cooking. What secret alche-

my or magic transformed simple ingredients into dishes so extraordinary? I needed to know, and sooner or later intended to find out. Meanwhile, I was happy enough just to enjoy them.

Le Cave di Maiano hooked us, and we never ventured beyond Maiano in our search for our picnic location. Luckily, someone in the restaurant knew of a house nearby that might suit us, and he took us to meet the caretaker of the property. The term "house" was a rather modest description for the Villa Maiano: a magnificent Renaissance palazzo, one grand reception room opening onto another even more impressive and, at the center, the most imposing of all—a huge double-story state room girdled by a handsome gallery. A plaque in the main hall commemorated Queen Victoria's stay, for the villa had been owned by an English aesthete and fellow watercolorist.

We thought the villa would be ideal for us. It was away from the city, it could easily accommodate all the paraphernalia of filmmaking, and the many rooms lent themselves to the sets we wanted for the pensione. The possibility now occurred to us of using a private house in the country as the pensione in the city.

The property belonged to the Contessa Lucrezia Corsini Miari Fulcis. The Corsinis are one of the oldest noble Italian families of whom it is said they could once walk from Florence to Rome without ever having to step off their own land. They sounded formidable. As the contessa was not in Florence at the time, the caretaker took us to the estate's olive press where we met the contessa's son, who promised to speak to her about our interest in the villa.

In the neighborhood of the villa we also found an ideal twisting drive for a carriage scene that features in the story, not far up the road from the art historian Bernard Berenson's famous villa, I Tatti. The alarming kiss could be staged against any of the spectacular valleys that surrounded us, though which of those valleys would yield up a carpet of flowers only spring would reveal.

Contessa Lucrezia Corsini Miari Fulcis

*M*ANY TIMES *I find myself alone somewhere in this big house of Maiano and it seems that these old walls are here to tell me the story of their life—and to echo the intense prayer, among these silences, of Santa Maria Maddalena dei Pazzi.*

I hear the voices still of the Tolomei, silk merchant Sir John Temple Leader, whose reconstruction of the house makes us see Maiano as it is today, and my uncles, the Storis, who never abandoned these walls during the war in 1944, and who loved them so much they never changed anything.

I love Maiano as it is, and so does my big family. But during the spring of 1986 something happened. We found ourselves invaded by the troupe of A Room with a View, and Maiano seemed to live again in an atmosphere that was left behind a hundred and fifty years ago. It was an extraordinary experience. The books, the suitcases, the china, the white linen, and everything that was needed, was already there in its place.

The actors, lying on the grass at the front of the villa having lunch, were like portraits of the past. It was as if John Temple Leader was there among them. Bravissimi, Benito the painter, Pizzonia the carpenter, and incredible Gianni Quaranta whose work revealed such great ability.

$\mathcal{B}$EFORE WE LEFT Florence, Elizabeth Marangoni invited us to dinner. I was greatly looking forward to a home-cooked Tuscan meal. Home-cooked food is usually far better than restaurant cooking, but the standard of Florentine restaurants was so impressive that I wondered how it could be improved on, even at home. I knew, of course, that Elizabeth was originally from New England and had moved to Florence on her marriage many years ago. So I was certain that we would be given fagioli rather than Boston baked beans.

Her son, Peter, came to drive us to their handsome eighteenth-century villa on the Pian de Guillari, a stunning hillside south of the city. The Marangoni house is a fine patrician villa built around a courtyard with an arched loggia at one end. Along one side of the house a broad terrace serves almost as an auditorium for the misty views of other faraway hills crowned with cypress, and valleys lined with olive trees. At the bottom one could see the Autostrada leading to Siena and points south, with its fast traffic. The gardens and the narrow paths that led to the orchards and olive groves were something I would have been happy to investigate further but for the bitter cold that quickly forced us inside.

I had never met Elizabeth before but I had heard so much about her from Peter that I felt I knew her well. A blazing log fire had been made for us in the mas-

Peter Marangoni and Elizabeth Marangoni, his mother, on the terrace of the Marangoni villa

Opposite:
Maggie Smith and Judi Dench

sive grate of the large drawing room. Elizabeth had prepared a wonderful dinner of pasta, beef in a wine sauce, and a variety of local cheeses served with salad. After dinner we sat by the fire drinking grappa and chatted for hours about Florence, about films and about food.

Peter offered to take us back to the hotel but not before detouring into the narrow streets behind the Piazza Signoria where we had coffee. Even at that late hour all the cafés were open, and the place buzzed promisingly with his friends and acquaintances—or acquaintances to be—where Peter was in his element.

I had met this immensely convivial man some years before through mutual friends in New York and liked him very much—good looking, intelligent, with a great sense of humor and an explosive laugh. He is an architect by profession, and although he lives and works mainly in New York, is a Florentine by birth and upbringing. When I knew we would be going to Florence to make the film, I thought it would be a perfect opportunity to recruit Peter for the Merchant Ivory team—in fact, an opportunity not to be wasted.

He became our associate producer and location manager on *A Room with a View* largely because I never gave him the option of refusing. And I have to admit that he was an excellent associate producer, even though he never allowed his duties on the film by day to interfere with his extensive social life. Every night, after shooting was over, he would be irresistibly drawn to the livelier piazzas, to pretty girls and to parties—and there he would still be in the early hours of the morning when the rest of us were getting ready to stumble sleepily to the set for the start of another day's filming.

WE HAD ONLY three months to set this picture up and thus far the only firm commitment we had was from British Screen. Roger Wingate of Curzon had shown a lot of interest, as had Channel 4, and we were also trying to get Goldcrest involved. But those deals were conditional on our finding an American distributor, which is always difficult for us as our films are not obviously commercial and therefore not immediately attractive to potential investors. Most of the distributors I approached weren't at all interested. Of the rest, some wanted to cast the film with American actors, others wanted to change the story line, and one even had doubts about the characters of Mr. Emerson and

Charlotte Bartlett because he thought the older characters were not that interesting to youthful audiences. Finally, Cinecom offered us an acceptable American deal, and we were able to proceed without compromising the integrity of Forster's novel, or his collection of Britishers abroad experiencing the joys and dangers of Italy.

For the part of Charlotte Bartlett we never considered anyone but Maggie Smith. Ever since she had worked with us on *Quartet* I had longed for the chance to work with her again. She was then in Congreve's *The Way of the World* at the Haymarket Theatre in London, and we sent the script to her there, where it arrived—and was this extraordinary coincidence or divine intervention?—at a very propitious moment. She was in her dressing room between the matinee and evening performance listening to a BBC radio adaptation of *A Room with a View* and received the script just as "her" dialogue was on the air.

> *But we fear him for you, dear. You are so young and inexperienced, you have lived among such nice people, that you cannot realize what men can be—how they can take a brutal pleasure in insulting a woman whom her sex does not protect and rally round. This afternoon, for example, if I had not arrived, what would have happened?*

I was no less single-minded in casting Judi Dench in the part of the eccentric novelist Eleanor Lavish. Twenty years earlier I had been in London for the release of our second film, Shakespeare Wallah, and saw this fine actress in a translation of the Russian play The Promise. Her interpretation of the dual role that she played so impressed me that I wrote her a fan letter expressing the wish that someday we would work together. Much to my surprise, she wrote back to say how much she had enjoyed our film and that she, too, hoped we might work together. We never imagined it would take twenty years.

Denholm Elliott was suggested by Celestia Fox, our casting director, to play the part of Mr. Emerson. He loved the script and immediately responded with enthusiasm. After a meeting with Jim, we cast him in the part.

We chose Patrick Godfrey to play the Reverend Eager and his wife, Amanda Walker, as the cockney Signora. They had both been in *Heat and Dust,* and over

the years they have become good friends of ours. The roles of the two elderly sisters, Teresa and Catherine Alan, went to Fabia Drake and Joan Henley. Both have since died, and it was good to have had the opportunity of working with these two distinguished ladies.

As we always do, we cast young unknown actors in the juvenile leads. We finally settled on Helena Bonham Carter as Lucy Honeychurch and Julian Sands as George Emerson. Helena had made only one film, but she had a special quality that set her apart from all the other young actresses we saw, so we took it on trust that she would be up to the demands of the role. Perhaps her lack of experience was even a positive virtue, and certainly her fresh beauty and intelligence recommended her. Julian was a somewhat more experienced actor, and his athleticism and unconventional, almost Slavic, brooding face seemed perfect for the muddled George.

Daniel Day Lewis came to see us straight from the set of *My Beautiful Launderette,* with parti-colored hair, and we liked him at once. He had the quality of "individual distinction" of appearance and personality that Jim looks for and relies on in casting as much as—or, sometimes, more than—an excellent audition. He would be the perfect Cecil Vyse.

We had long wanted to work with Simon Callow and felt he would make a very good Reverend Beebe. But when he received the script, he thought he had been offered the part of George Emerson. When I set him straight, he professed to be disappointed that we weren't considering him for the young leading man, and it took some persuading by Jim to convince him. The argument Jim is supposed to have used on him is that if he were to play the Reverend Beebe it would be so much less boring than if anyone else were to do it. So he had to accept. We hadn't, however, bargained for the fresh and livid scar that decorated his face when he arrived in Florence. I was very concerned, and asked him how it had happened. "Crete," he said. "Eight stitches. I fell off a motor bike. Stupid thing to do." I agreed with

Fabia Drake [left] and Joan Henley

him. "Simon, when you are about to star in your first film, it is very stupid indeed to fall off a motor bike." "No, Ismail," he replied. "Falling *off* the bike was an accident. Getting *on* it was stupid. Ever seen what passes for a road in Crete?"

At the same time, we began to assemble the crew. We needed two assistant directors, one English and one Italian. We were very fortunate to have Pippo Pisciotto as the latter. Charming and liked by everyone, he had worked with Zeffirelli on many films. It was Pippo who recommended the Italian designer Gianni Quaranta as our production designer. Kevin Barker, the first assistant director on *Heat and Dust,* was Pippo's English counterpart. It went without saying that Jenny Beavan and John Bright would design the costumes as they have for so many of our films before and since.

Jim wanted to use a new cinematographer. He thinks he gets lazy using the same ones over and over. He had already decided that he didn't want Florence to be made to look picturesque or, God forbid, pretty. There is always a danger with visually stunning places of producing a too sentimentally pleasing effect. We had seen Tony Pierce-Roberts's work on *A Private Function,* which he had deliberately shot with a stark postwar feel that was both attractively spare and formally satisfying. We met with Tony, and when he told me that one of the many reasons he wanted to do the film was because he was looking forward to all those wonderful Tuscan meals, I knew I hadn't the heart to refuse.

With everything now falling into place, our second recce to Florence in mid-March was an introduction for Tony Pierce-Roberts and Gianni Quaranta into the low-budget production methods of Merchant Ivory. Here were vast spaces to light—but not the wherewithal to provide the lighting equipment Tony was used to. Here was a room—perhaps—but with no view. We took them to the Piazza Signoria to show Tony the human obstacles—hundreds of tourists of every nationality and disposition—around which he would have to shoot, while Gianni was left to ponder the thorny problem of the nonexistent view.

TONY PIERCE-ROBERTS (CINEMATOGRAPHER)

I'M ALWAYS AMAZED *when I hear other people's accounts of their experience on films on which I've also worked. In the case of* A Room with a View, *where was I when they were soaking up the atmosphere of the countryside in*

Fiesole, or gorging cuisine à l'indienne, or shopping with Ismail? Was I on the same picture?

The answer, of course, is that I was in the trenches with a motley group of rather bemused Italians (all mysteriously titled macchinistas), with little communication between us since Ismail believes translators are for wimps.

When I arrived in Florence to start filming, the weather had become very bad: gray skies, endless rain—very British, in fact. The schedule was changed to take advantage of this, and so we started with the scene in which Maggie Smith, Denholm Elliott, Helena Bonham Carter, and the others return by carriage to Florence during a violent thunderstorm after their picnic in the hills.

We put the camera on the top of a wooded hill in order to film the passing carriages, and then we waited until the Florentine fire brigade laid out all their hoses to provide consistent "movie" rain as the real stuff came and went rather fitfully. My English camera crew were all sensibly equipped with the appropriate wet-weather gear and were all set to shoot when one of the macchinistas stood in front of the camera and said we couldn't shoot because his crew would get wet. It was explained to him that rain was the whole purpose of the scene, that it was in the script, and anyway, why didn't they have macs? He said that it was his union's position that the company should provide appropriate wet-weather clothing. Ismail went into one of his "In thirty years I have never had to . . ." speeches but eventually someone was dispatched to Florence to get some waterproof macs for the Italian crew. All the messenger could find, alas, were the "tourist specials"—a very thin multicolored, plastic packamack, that ripped on contact with any flexed muscle.

When we were all suitably attired, we looked like a variety pack of colored condoms, but at least shooting could commence. "Shoot, Jim, shoot," cried Ismail as the fire brigade released a deluge that almost washed the carriages, horses, and actors off the road and into the forest. In doing so they used up their entire water supply for the day on the first take. While some of his men went off to find more water, we told the chief fireman that we didn't need a typhoon, just ordinary rain. Yes, yes, he said, but the fire brigade thought this was an ideal practice exercise for their trainee firemen.

After many attempts, we achieved the shot and slid down the hill to have lunch. Normally, film companies provide catering facilities for film crews on location, and Ismail had unearthed some airline catering firm that provided a packed lunch that included horrid cardboard cartons of equally horrid cardboard wine. The usually jolly

Helena Bonham Carter and
Julian Sands

faces of my macchinistas fell into their boots, and one of the crew came to me and said mournfully, "Tony, this is food for babies." After much muttering amongst themselves, the Italians approached Ismail and Peter Marangoni and struck a deal. Ismail agreed to provide cash to one of the Italian drivers who would be responsible for organizing lunch for the Italian crew, and Ismail would make other arrangements for the rest of the party.

A friendly spirit of competition then evolved as we began a succession of the most glorious al fresco meals I've ever eaten. Unknown to us, the Italian driver owned a restaurant and provided such delights as barbecued steaks, penne all'arrabiata, and one day (again a rather damp one), a memorable spaghetti—with chips.

Inevitably, more and more of the English crew sidled toward the "Italian lines." Occasionally even Ismail himself, who, having entertained the cast to one of his own specially created recipes, would furtively slip round the corner for "seconds."

*S*O, HAVING introduced them to the worst they could expect, we then took them to the Villa Maiano. Given our four-week shooting schedule, time was a very important consideration, and cameraman and art director both agreed that shooting at the country villa was a very good idea. The spaces there meant that they could work in an unrestricted way and save a lot of time. Beyond that, the estate contained wonderful places for exterior scenes of every kind except those strictly urban ones in downtown Florence. Thus the work could be efficiently contained.

After the morning recce at Maiano we returned to the city where everyone rushed off to enjoy a wonderful five-course lunch at some fine restaurant. Peter had frequently told me about the tripe carts in Florence, which are rather like the hot-dog stands in New York, and this was a good opportunity to sample this speciality in a typically Florentine way. He took me to the Piazza dei Cimatori, a tiny square just behind the Piazza Signoria. In the middle of the square was a colorful wooden street cart shaded by an umbrella. This particular tripe-pitch was over a hundred years old, an institution in Florence, and was owned by Miro Pinzauti. Most people do not consider tripe any kind of delicacy—just the opposite. But if you come from Bombay, where it is a speciality, you have no qualms about such snacks.

I had heard Peter describe Pinzauti's many times but it was impossible to imagine—it's something that needs to be seen and experienced. The raw tripe is actually stewed on the cart and kept in heated buckets, then chopped and served with a wonderful salsa verde in a large rustic bun. It was absolutely delicious.

Now that we had decided the Villa Maiano suited everyone, I arranged to meet the contessa to see if she would allow us to shoot in it. As the relatively paltry amount of money we could pay her for giving us permission to shoot on her property clearly would not be a consideration in this case, we had to hope that the idea itself would appeal to her.

We were not coming as great movie moguls because our films were hardly known in Italy at that time. After traveling there over the years and getting to know Italians, I always felt they would respond favorably to our films. But although the Italian critics and journalists who saw our films at Cannes and other festivals were enthusiastic about them, for a long time they never crusaded on our behalf or made any effort to persuade Italian distributors to buy them. *Quartet* was our first to be dubbed into Italian and released there—seventeen years after the Italian critics had seen *Shakespeare Wallah* to which they had reacted so sympathetically. *Quartet* was followed by *Heat and Dust*, which played very successfully in Italy, and on the strength of that, I thought we might be able to interest an Italian investor in *A Room with a View*. But neither the Italian distributors nor RAI, the major television company, would commit. Since the successful release of *A Room with a View* in Italy, the whole character of our relationship with Italian audiences has changed. The country has become one of our most lucrative territories, and a source of major support for our work, which now has a devoted following there. All this was to come; meanwhile we had to convince the contessa.

Luckily, she was intrigued by our proposal. She had read the novel and liked it very much, so she was enthusiastic about the project, and was more generous toward us than we could ever have expected. We got along extremely well. She was youthful and spontaneous, and I was surprised that she had grown-up children who were already out doing things in the world, for she scarcely looked any older than they did.

The next problem facing us was obtaining permission to shoot in the Piazza Signoria. The officials we had spoken to before had wanted to know how many square meters of the piazza we would need and for how many minutes—and *that* wasn't the kind of arrangement I had in mind at all. What we needed was to have the square—all of it—totally cleared for two days.

Only the mayor of Florence, Lando Conti, could grant us wholesale access to the piazza and other parts of the city, while Santa Croce was in the province of the holy fathers. Peter, who knew the mayor, had already approached him on this matter, and he now arranged a meeting between the three of us. I was told that in the hierarchy of Italy the mayor of Florence ranks as the second most important man in the country. He received us with great civility and explained why, alas, he could not grant our request. But we continued talking, and during the conversation we told him that the novel had been translated into Italian by Marisa Caramella who was the ex-mayor's wife (and whom we had, in fact, asked to put in a good word for us). The mayor knew the whole family very well, he said, and then, somehow or other, we began to discuss food. He was surprised to hear from Peter that I often cook for the cast and crew during filming, and we invited him to come and visit the set and eat with us.

By the time we left the mayor's office he had, seemingly, agreed to let us have as much of the Piazza Signoria—or any other piazza—as we wanted and for as long as we wanted. This was very good news indeed, but I kept it a secret from Jim. In fact, I told him that the mayor had only granted us permission to use the square for a day and a half. Directors need to feel a certain urgency when they venture into the heart of a great city with their army. If I had told Jim the truth, he would still be in the Piazza Signoria today shooting the same scene he began seven years ago.

Then we had another stroke of good fortune. Peter remembered a friend of his who had an apartment along the Oltrarno, that is to say on the south bank of the river facing the city. He recalled that the apartment had exactly the kind of Florentine view we sought. It was not the view Lucy Honeychurch saw when she traded her room with the Emersons; that view no longer existed. It was better.

We went to see it and the view from the south bank turned out to be our classic view. One could see the Duomo, Giotto's bell tower, and the tower of the Palazzo Signoria, the Uffizi, Santa Croce—and there was just enough distance to blur the evidence of the late twentieth century. It was perfect except for one flaw: in order to see this magnificent cityscape you had to lean far out of the window. As we needed to show first Lucy, then later on Lucy and George together, framed by the window with the view of the city in the background, there seemed no way to take the shot. Gianni Quaranta, however, considered the large terrace on one side of the apartment and decided he could mock up a room there; so that, although

Overleaf: The Arno from the Altrarno

we would be shooting from the terrace outside, the effect would be as from inside a room. The window, the curtains, the wallpaper, the furniture—all would frame the view, and no one would be the wiser. So this elaborate trick became the view of the film, the publicity posters, book and record covers, and all the rest. No wonder tourists are frustrated when they try to find it at the Pensione Quisisana, or any other pensione on the north bank of the Arno.

HELENA BONHAM CARTER (LUCY HONEYCHURCH)

From my experience, most producers of the orthodox kind rarely make an appearance on the set during filming, and when they do they hover inconspicuously in the background looking worried but content to leave the creative side and actual business of filmmaking to the director. With Ismail this is never the case because he is hardly orthodox. I remember him as a constant presence; anxious to further the process along in any way, his activity may be best described as a very conscientious usher. With every best intention Ismail is, or was at least on A Room with a View, very much a back-seat driver producer.

He charmed (by buying them ice cream) the hordes of disgruntled and uncomprehending tourists who had traveled from afar to see the Piazza Signoria only to be faced by an Indian gentleman explaining to them that they could not because he owned it for the day. As indeed he did—because the only way to film in any Florentine square was by renting it by the square meter from the town council.

The last shot of the film, where the newly married Lucy and George are kissing against the eponymous view, seems wistfully romantic but was treacherous to film. Julian Sands and I found ourselves perched precariously on a parapet inside a free-standing window frame (courtesy of the Art Department) with a direct hundred-foot drop into the Arno below. While Jim suggested, "I think both of you can afford a bit more passion," Ismail was on the other side of the Arno stopping cars. This he did simultaneous to persuading shopkeepers to turn off their neon signs and discouraging innocent shoppers from emerging with their goods. From our vantage point we saw the diminutive though recognizably animated figure of Ismail jumping up and down, arms waving, and heard his familiar exhortation, "Shoot, Jim, for God's sake SHOOT," rising above all the other noises of the Florentine rush hour.

Ismail is an essentially creative person whose super-abundance of energy as a pro-

ducer, however creative his financing may be, is sometimes frustrated by willful directors, actors, and writers. The area in which it is allowed full expression and release is in the kitchen. In Florence he cooked and fed the entire crew several times, serving it up al fresco in the romantically dilapidated gardens of the Villa Maiano. At the end of the week any waning morale or stress incurred by low-budget conditions were restored and soothed by generous portions of dal and basmati rice.

"Ismail invites you to cuisine à l'Indienne after wrap," the previous day's call sheet would announce. But the truth is, his cooking is as unorthodox and unconventionally "Indian" as his producing. Just as his films are hybrids of nationalities, his dishes are often a cosmopolitan mix of Eastern spices with ingredients indigenous to whichever country he finds himself in. A vital part of the cooking is the shopping for the food. His cooking is wholesomely delicious, unfussy and informed by a basic respect for the ingredients. Although producing films and food may seem quite disparate vocations, with Ismail the methods are similar. He is speedy to the point of instantaneous; he cooks and invents new concoctions by improvisation, using his wits and trusting his instincts, measurements determined by taste rather than precise scientific means. And he is miraculously resourceful. On one occasion, arriving back at his flat with no less than ten guests arriving in an hour, we were faced with a starkly empty cupboard save frugal amounts of rice, mustard, peas, and potatoes. Ismail started up quite blithely and produced a feast that little betrayed his resources. He knows how to make a little go a long way, in the kitchen and on the screen.

That is not to say Ismail is stingy. By nature he is an expansive and generous spirit; a tireless enthusiast of all that is delicious and good in life; an epicure of things celluloid or edible; a culinary alchemist and professional catalyst who galvanizes others into doing and provides the situation in which they can do it. Fueled by an essential desire to share, to give pleasure to others, and to entertain, Ismail is a life-enhancer who improves the quality of life for the many who like his films and the fortunate few who are invited to dinner.

$\mathcal{E}$XACTLY THREE MONTHS since our first recce we were on the Maiano hillside with the cameras ready to roll, even though the weather was very much against us. It was gray and rainy and, as it had been pouring with rain in the previous days, the ground had turned to slushy mud. The trucks got

stuck, the costumes got muddy, and no one thought we would be able to get a decent shot that first day. But we could not afford to lose that day's precious shooting hours because of the bad weather, so we went ahead anyway and hoped for the best. Our first shot was of Julian Sands racing downhill in a rain storm, his arms outstretched in a kind of ecstasy induced by love and wild weather.

It was a good start, but the long-term weather forecast was for more rain, so we hastily rearranged the week's schedule. We had planned to shoot exteriors first in order to give the art department time to prepare the interiors, but now, ready or not, we had no option but to move inside. Fortunately, Gianni had already completed the bedrooms so we could reschedule the scenes we would shoot after lunch on that first wet day.

Our first lunch on the *Room with a View* set should have been a very special occasion. I have always taken a personal interest in the catering on my films, and whatever else we may have to skimp, I try not to compromise on the quality or quantity of the food. In this instance, and because of the Italian connection, everyone, including myself, expected the quality of the catering to surpass even my own demanding standards. So when the catering truck arrived, I was shocked to see that it was piled high with prepacked polystyrene boxes of the fast-food sort. It wasn't just the shocking manner of the presentation but that inside each box was an unappetizing heap of congealed and sweating pasta and an overcooked slab of something that might or might not have been meat.

I was very disappointed and ashamed because this really wasn't what we had expected. Obviously, these were not the best caterers in Florence and they would have to be swiftly replaced, but I was told that any professional caterer would produce the same miserable result. Italians respect their food too much to accept the idea of anyone handling it as a mere commodity. Prepared mass catering is anathema to them, and moreover, the very nature of Italian food makes such a process a practical impossibility. As Italy has a flourishing film industry, and not all those films are made at Cinecittà nor do the crews fast for the duration of filming, it seemed a good idea to find out how the Italians deal with this problem.

Italian crews are given an allowance for lunch, and they go to a local trattoria. This was fine for the crew, but getting actors out of their cumbersome Edwardian costumes and corsets before a trattoria lunch and back into them afterward would add another hour to the working day, and that was time we did not have—for they could hardly be expected to roam around the city looking for a place to eat in a

A cast picnic lunch

37

state of dress that might be perceived as mildly eccentric. So, how could the cast be fed?

The answer, of course, was all around us—in the kaleidoscopic displays of fresh fruit and vegetables at the markets, in the enormous variety of cold meats and cheeses at the salumeria, and in the tempting aroma of baking breads from the forno. We could have picnics—fabulous picnics that no one would ever forget. This task was taken on by Lindsey Lee, Jim's personal assistant from Boston, and my nephew Nayeem Hafizka, who had come from Bombay to help on the film.

The actors liked the idea. They all said that with the prospect of so many fine restaurants to explore in the evenings they didn't want to eat too much in the middle of the day. There was little sign of this restraint during the picnics, though, when they would heap all the different salads and any amount of salami and cold chicken onto their plates, which they then wiped clean with the last crumbs of bread.

Besides the daily picnic, a succession of little treats would appear throughout the day to keep everyone going: fruit, biscuits, and crusty freshly baked bread filled with different kinds of ham, salami, or meat and tomatoes and olives. This made the actors' lot—the tiresome hanging around and waiting with nothing to do—a little more bearable. I remember one day apologizing to Denholm Elliott for the long delay before he was called to do his scene. "Well, Ismail," he replied cheerfully, "we're standing on this beautiful mountainside; fragrant cypresses all around; a view of Florence in the distance; sunlight; barn swallows flying around this lovely old farmhouse; drinking espresso coffee and eating these excellent sandwiches—and getting paid for it. What could be nicer."

The preoccupation with food began so quietly at first that it was almost imperceptible; just the normal hum at the end of the day's shooting about who was eating where and with whom. Gradually it grew: the buzz became louder, started earlier, became more insistent. Then the matter of where to dine became very serious: restaurants were discussed, comparisons made, discoveries recommended and addresses exchanged.

The inevitable shop talk over a film-set lunch now completely changed character. It seemed more like a seminar on the comparative merits of the various eating places and chefs in the city. And in the cold light of dawn, a time of day when the most one can expect from a film unit is that they drag their bodies to the set as per their contracts, everyone would be joyously discussing where and what they had eaten the night before.

As for me, I was torn between trying out every restaurant in the city and revisiting all those I had been to before. Whenever I had an urge to return to a restaurant I already knew, I would justify this less adventurous option by taking with me someone who had not been there. Which is how I came to invite Maggie Smith to dine with me at Coco Lezzone.

The front door of Coco Lezzone opens into a tiny white-walled room furnished in its entirety with two tables and a couple of benches. There is no other adornment whatsoever. At this point most people coming here for the first time back out into the street, assuming they've made a terrible mistake and walked into someone's kitchen, or worse, perhaps into a men's room in a public building.

SIMON CALLOW (REVEREND BEEBE)

*I*SMAIL FIRST *asked me to act for him in* Heat and Dust *and I couldn't accept because the play I was doing in London obstinately remained on. By way of consolation, Ismail announced, "I will make a film for you—you will play the leading part."*

True to his word, three years later he phoned me and said, "Now we've made this script for you—your film—and it will be wonderful. I'm sending the script." The package arrived; I tore it open, and there was the script for A Room with a View. *I read it with increasing excitement because as this was, according to Ismail, my film, I naturally assumed that the part of George Emerson was my part, and I was amazed at Ismail's imagination. He saw me as I saw myself—a romantic and passionate and, possibly, tragic individual. But at the back of my mind there must have been a doubt because I phoned my agent to confirm that it was the part of George they wanted me for. It wasn't. It was the part of Reverend Beebe. "Tell him no," I said. "I won't do it."*

Ismail immediately phoned to ask why I had turned down the role that would be so wonderful for me. I was so hurt, so profoundly upset I just told him it wasn't right for me. His response was to invite me to a cocktail party he was giving.

There were dozens of illustrious people at the party, and Ismail introduced me to each guest as "Simon Callow, who is playing the Reverend Beebe for us." "No, Ismail," I corrected him each time, "I am not going to play the Reverend Beebe." And, every

*time, Ismail just smiled knowingly and said, "Oh, but he will." I had no idea then of
Ismail's childlike capacity for stubbornly holding his breath until everyone caves in and
he gets his own way.*

*After the party Ismail phoned again to confirm that I was going to play Reverend
Beebe. "No, Ismail, I'm not going to play Reverend Beebe." So he invited me to breakfast. Over curry croissants I listened to how wonderful I would be in the role of Reverend Beebe. "No, Ismail."*

*This pantomime-style contradiction and counter-contradiction went on for some
weeks until, completely punch-drunk, I heard myself quietly say "yes"—at which Ismail
nearly keeled over.*

*I never intended to play Reverend Beebe, but I'm awfully glad I did because,
although I didn't understand anything at all about film acting at that time, it's probably the film performance most people remember and like above all the others I've given.*

Ismail, typically, was right. Though—contrary to his claim—it wasn't for my ben-efit that he made the film. I suspect Ismail's true motive for making a film in Italy was gastronomic rather than cinematic, and the filming of A Room with a View *was just a cover under which he could shamelessly indulge his inexhaustible passion for food. We all ate well in Florence, often at Ismail's trough, more often at one of the many excel-lent restaurants that Ismail has such a gift for discovering.*

On the day we had successfully completed what was my longest scene in the film, Ismail decided we should celebrate with dinner at the best restaurant in Florence. "Come," he commanded, indicating a restaurant on the hillside that I'd seen and noted as potentially rather wonderful. "It is," he confirmed, "the best restaurant in Florence."

Ismail, exploding with energy and charisma, led us into the restaurant. But they didn't want us; they were full. An ugly altercation followed and Ismail marched out, reassuring his troops that there was another restaurant farther down the hill where they knew him well and it was, in fact, "the best restaurant in Florence." So we obediently followed him there, but they were full, too. Nothing daunted, Ismail told us there was yet another "best restaurant in Florence" at the bottom of the hill. That one was shut. "Never mind," said Ismail. "There are other places—many, many, many places in Florence."

So we crossed the Arno and marched behind him along unknown narrow streets until we arrived right in the heart of the city and fetched up at some absolutely filthy, foul dive, which, not surprisingly, was empty, open, and seemed to want our custom. Ismail announced, with what seemed to me extraordinarily misplaced triumph, "We have finally arrived at the very best restaurant in Florence and we will eat here and it will be wonderful." And, against all the evidence, it was. It turned out to be absolute-ly fabulous and every dish we ate was more wonderful than the one before.

Ismail had never been to this place before, never even seen it or knew it existed. But he had decided that we would eat at "the best restaurant in Florence" that night, and we did. Though whether it was by chance or whether it was the sheer force of Ismail's will that rendered the seediest dive in Florence a temple where Epicure might worship will always remain a mystery.

ON THE NIGHT I took Maggie, this first room was jammed with a crowd of animated eaters packed elbow to elbow on the benches.

Maggie's expression told me that this was definitely not what she had expected, and sensing her disinclination to remain and expecting one of her famous drawled asides, I indicated the second, larger room beyond, which was just as packed but where a table had been specially reserved for us.

In Florence if you visit a restaurant more than once you are considered a regular; more than twice and you are greeted as a friend. By now I had become a habitué of Coco Lezzone so the owner himself, Franco Paoli, came and discussed the menu with us, proposed some wines we might like to try and made us feel very comfortable and welcome. Maggie was absolutely delighted with the food, and we had a very enjoyable evening, but I was glad she never asked me what the name Coco Lezzone meant: unfortunately, it translates as "the dirty cook."

Despite the traffic our film unit generated in the city's restaurants every night, it was nevertheless rare for one group to collide with another in the same place. It happened to me only once, and on a Sunday night when many of the better-known restaurants are closed, so that the chances of avoiding people you know are considerably reduced.

Richard Robbins, my close friend and the composer of the music for all our films since 1979, arrived in Florence and I asked Peter Marangoni to recommend a really good restaurant where we could take him. Peter suggested we should go to Cammillo, but he was rather concerned that, not having made a reservation much earlier, we would not get a table on a Sunday night. I told him to take us there and to let me worry about getting a table.

There was a long line of people waiting outside the restaurant. We were too hungry and impatient to join the queue, and I went inside and asked to speak with the owner. I told him that I was a very important food writer and had come to Florence specifically to write about his restaurant. Most Florentine restaurateurs don't care what is written about them because they all know how good their food is, so the owner wasn't impressed by that; but he was concerned that I had, apparently, come all the way from India just to eat at his restaurant. He said there was a tiny table at the back of the room, and if we didn't mind the shortage of space, we could sit there.

After we had sat down at the tiny table, I saw Maggie and her husband, Beverly Cross, at the entrance being motioned to wait in the line. I couldn't allow my star to stand in the street while her producer sat inside, so even though our table could

barely accommodate three people let alone five, I called them over to join us. She squeezed herself in somehow, famous wrists and famous elbows working, and drawled, "Cozy."

SOMEHOW, BETWEEN the breakfasts and lunches, and the lunches and dinners, the film was being made. Coincidentally, the weather changed exactly on cue as we completed the interior shooting, and one of the wettest springs suddenly gave way to one of the hottest summers. By the middle of May the temperature was already ninety degrees and, instead of hanging around the set, many of the actors took advantage of any free time to explore the countryside outside Florence.

We were all dispersed in different hotels around the city, and some of the production team even ended up living at the Villa Maiano because there was no more room in the jam-packed hotels. Fortunately, we had established such a good relationship with the contessa that she permitted those few members of the team to stay at the villa, and to sleep in the vast Napoleonic beds. Thus they also acted as security guards for the costumes and props the contessa allowed us to house there.

The Quisisana was our base, and at some point in the evening we would all congregate there. The proprietress, Virginia Marasco, made it her business to look after us with true Italian hospitality, and one evening she persuaded her husband, the musician Riccardo Marasco, a specialist in seventeenth-century Italian music, to come to the Quisisana and play for us. This was a particular treat for Dick Robbins who was fascinated by the original instruments, especially the *chitarra-lyra,* the precursor of the modern guitar.

At this time Dick was considering various musical possibilities for the sound track. Ultimately, and aside from his own original compositions, he chose arias by Puccini, and the popularity of the film made Puccini's *O Mio Babbino Caro* and *Chi Il Bel Sogno Di Doretta* even more widely recognized—until the 1990 World Cup brought *Nessun Dorma* to the public.

Those arias from *Gianni Schicchi* and *La Rondine* became so closely associated with the film that Puccini's connection with them was entirely overshadowed. Kiri te Kanawa, whose performance of them we used on the track, once appeared on an American talk show where she was asked to sing the "Room with a View" song. When she asked which of the two Puccini arias they wanted, she was told no *Puccini* arias please, just the "Room with a View" song.

RICHARD ROBBINS (COMPOSER)

I HAD TWO *official reasons for being in Florence for the shooting of* A Room with a View: *the first was to soak up the general atmosphere of the countryside, research the music of the place and period and so on; the second was to rehearse Helena Bonham Carter for her two scenes in the film when she plays some quite difficult pieces on the piano. What an assignment!*

I arrived well-armed with the tools of my trade: scores of Beethoven and Schubert for Helena, and a Walkman for me, with lots of cassettes. Helena and I had spoken very briefly in London before the shooting began. We had principally discussed the Beethoven selection. But the real work and fun was scheduled to begin in Florence, before and after shooting hours. This was very demanding for her because she appeared in nearly every scene shot in Florence. Her schedule was far busier than mine, so I had a lot of time for "research," and this often meant wandering around the hills of Fiesole with my Walkman on my head listening to—well, what did I listen to? Beethoven, Schubert, Tchaikovsky, Bach, lots of arias, naturally, by Verdi and Puccini, and a variety of lesser-known composers. I also spent some time, very legitimately, poring over turn-of-the-century sheet music, which I found in Florentine collections with the kind help of Elizabeth Marangoni, who knows the city like the palm of her hand.

Helena and I worked out the necessary passages for the shooting. She practiced faithfully, long and hard, and was, in fact, an inspiration, always positive and capable of total concentration even when exhausted. After work was all over for the day we abandoned ourselves to the delights of the kitchen and dining room.

Though there was often a great deal of restaurant-going, there was also a lot of cooking going on in the kitchen of the Villa Maiano. The kitchen of this very grand and wonderful villa, though ill equipped by American standards, was capable of producing the most wonderful delights. This was, I believe, because of easy access to very superior ingredients, not the least of which was the olive oil from the estate, and also because of Ismail's energy and imagination, and of his having a number of very capable and enthusiastic assistants (myself included).

One of the more dedicated followers at the time was Lindsey Lee from Boston, who managed to produce out of this kitchen lunches, teas, snacks, and evening suppers, which were quite remarkable for their lavishness, yet with none of the advantages of a modern kitchen. Using her own imagination, and Ismail's directives, she was forever presenting us with delightful surprises. We were always saying "How did she ever do this? Where did she find such and such? She knows all the markets, every one!" The breads and salads, fruits, cheeses—well, it went on and on. And continually, through all this, the filmmaking and all the thousands of related logistical bits of business, there was Ismail, tasting, testing, cooking, sampling, ordering, criticizing, encouraging, shouting curses and praises. What a glorious time it was for us all.

Recently, on a return visit over six years later, it seemed to me that absolutely nothing had changed. Everything looked, smelled, and sounded the same, except that the excitement of the activity of filming A Room with a View was, of course, missing.

We revisited a number of the locations where we had shot, including the Villa Maiano, where everything seemed to be locked in a peaceful dreamlike state, under a bell jar. The season was high summer and it was quite hot, the cicadas were making an incredible racket but the kind that makes one want to doze off in a hammock. We wandered around in the blazing sun in the garden next to the Orangery at Maiano. I found myself looking for a tortoise that Helena and I had found in that walled garden six years before. I didn't find it, but I am very sure that it was there.

$\mathcal{A}$LTHOUGH THE WEATHER was now ideal for exterior shooting, the conditions were still treacherous. The heavy and persistent rain had made a swamp of the countryside, but we just had to make the best of it. For the crew these conditions meant the constant pushing and hauling of heavy vehicles that inevitably became embedded in the mud. I chipped in to help whenever necessary, and that created an immediate camaraderie with the Italian crew, which was one of the best I have ever worked with. They were hard working, cheerful, dedicated, and on most occasions, flexible. Of course there were many disagreements: when Italians get angry they get very angry and explode all over the place, but then it's finished and you are friends again. The Italian temperament is similar to my own, so we understood each other. And Italian arguments seem not always to be about establishing winners and losers, or rights and wrongs—but, rather, a civilized way of airing grievances over another glass of wine.

Helena Bonham Carter and Lucca
Rossi, the carriage driver, on the set

The crew cooking their own meal

Whenever we worked at locations that were far from any trattoria, the Italian crew would provide their own picnics—which were far more interesting and elaborate than ours. Sometimes they would build a fire and we would be drawn there by the aromas of grilled meat. We were always asked to join them, and that is how we discovered all sorts of wonderful peasant dishes, like bruschetta—toasted chunks of country bread brushed generously with olive oil and garlic and heaped with fresh chopped tomatoes—and the famous Florentine speciality, Bistecca alla Fiorentina, huge T-bone steaks cooked over a wood fire, which gives the meat its very distinctive taste.

Sometimes I repaid their hospitality when we were shooting at the Villa, and I would invade the kitchen to cook spaghetti with tomato sauce à l'Indienne for them. The Italians found it a refreshing change to have a film producer cook for the crew, but from my point of view it was no more novel than to have the grips and electricians cook for me.

Our unit now also included the two old horse carriages and their drivers who usually worked in the city giving rides around Florence to the tourists. We needed the carriages for the film, and when we met Lucca Rossi, the owner of one of the carriages, we thought his face was so interesting that we offered him the part of the coach driver; whereupon Lucca brought along his partner to be the driver of the second carriage. After the release of the film Lucca and his carriage became something of a tourist attraction, and frequently he would be offered double or triple the usual rate because of *Camera Con Vista*.

$\mathcal{W}$E HAD ALL BEEN holding our breaths for the first day of shooting at the Piazza Signoria. We had no idea of what to expect, nor of whether we would be able to pull it off, and Jim admits today that he and his cameraman had absolutely no plan beyond making use of a very expensive crane imported from Rome. We arrived at the piazza soon after dawn. It was deserted and chilly, but above the cold stone of the buildings I could see the sky turning into a brilliant blue: that rich, deep, almost dark blue that always heralds a perfect day. I hoped it was an omen. We had prayed for a cessation of rain on the two days we'd rented the square, and it appeared our prayer had been answered.

Flimsy metal barriers had already been erected around the perimeter of the

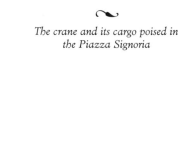

square, and gradually the unit began to arrive. By the time we were ready to shoot, at nine o'clock, large crowds had gathered beyond the barriers. Access to the square was blocked, but the people who lived in the city had to go about their business, and we had no idea how they would take all this. As for the tourists—well, I really don't know what they made of it. They conscientiously took their photographs, but I wonder if they were aware that this was not a characteristic representation of the Piazza Signoria. On the other hand, most tourists consider it a bonus to find a film crew and a hundred costumed extras on one of the regular guide-book beats, and they enjoy the novelty. The slides they take and show back home to friends are far more glamorous, and they look forward to seeing the film when it comes out.

But the moment that the expensive Roman crane was finally in position, with its valuable cargo of cameraman, director, assistant cameraman, and Panavision camera poised a hundred feet above the costumed strolling extras, one of those demonstrations erupted that Latin countries know so well. The demonstrators were housewives, carrying large placards, and they positioned themselves so that the camera could not fail to include them in any scene shot that day. The housewives were demanding better housing, and they hoped their message would get across via our camera, which they mistook for television.

In India we have many such demonstrations. They erupt suddenly, there is noise, pushing and shoving, high-pitched argument and then—like a sudden storm, it's all over. This felt like the same sort of thing to me, and at home I would have reasoned with the housewives, soothed them, made them promises, introduced them to my stars, and sent them on their way. But these chants were in Italian, we had no stars that day, and so my ingenuity would be tested.

Peter and I began to talk to the demonstrators. I explained to them that I had come all the way from India to make this film, and that I was very surprised by this disruptive demonstration because in India everyone is very cooperative and completely silent when you are making a film in a public place, and perhaps it would be a good idea to go somewhere and talk about it. In a little lane leading into the square I had noticed a series of pizzarias serving different kinds of pizzas, schiaccata, and other covered breads, so I suggested we should go there and I would treat everyone to pizzas. Peter thought that might do the trick. The demonstrators got very excited about this and began to follow me there. We all had huge square slices of pizza and enjoyed them very much, and the demonstrators seemed to forget all about their demonstration. But the peace lasted only as long as the pizzas, where-

The Piazza Signoria during a shoot

upon the demonstrators thanked me, returned to the square and started demonstrating again.

Despite that, all the scenes at the Piazza Signoria and at Santa Croce went off very well—except for a mishap of our own making. We were about to shoot the scene where Charlotte Bartlett and Lucy Honeychurch meet the novelist Eleanor Lavish in the Piazza Signoria on the day after the murder had taken place there. Typically, we were using stand-ins for the actors while we set up and lit the shot. During one of the rehearsals a flock of pigeons flew by, and Jim liked the effect so much that he wanted it in the shot, but of course there was no way we could communicate that to the pigeons. So I bought some peanuts and wherever I scattered them the pigeons would fly there. Attracting swarms of pigeons has become something of a speciality for me on our films—I now do it as professionally as any propman and his beaters.

When everything was ready and the actors were called, I hid behind a column in the Loggia dei Lanzi to be out of shot, but in the right direction to tempt the pigeons with the nuts. As soon as I heard Jim shout "action," I tossed a handful of peanuts high into the air and, perfectly on cue, a flock of pigeons swooped across Maggie's path, almost taking her hat with them. I saw her flicking her elegant wrists at them maniacally and heard her shouting "shoo" and "go away" and realized that no one had told Maggie what we had planned, so, of course, she had been taken by surprise. Unfortunately, that was one of the sequences that was cut from the film.

Jenny Beavan's wardrobe base was in a street near the Piazza dell' Indipendenza and conveniently close to our city locations—as the crow flies. By car, though, it was a complicated process through a maze of one-way streets and other prohibitions. The shooting at the Piazza Signoria required a large number of extras. We arranged a bus to ferry them to the location after they had been dressed. Because this journey would have to be repeated many times, we began very early in the morning. Even so, during the first trip I could see that this system would take us too long and we would never get all the extras to the piazza in time. So on the next journey I told the driver to ignore the one-way signs and just drive in a straight line. This he did without argument—in fact, with some glee. There was hardly any traffic at first, but with each trip the traffic increased and the journey became more hair-raising as we dodged this way and that along the narrow streets.

When Jenny had dressed the last extra, I put her on the bus and we charged right through the oncoming traffic. She went completely white and got out and refused to ride on the bus at all. She went back and forth on foot, until she finally staggered into the piazza with the last load of hats and umbrellas. She looked as though all the energy had been sapped from her, so I went into one of the cafés and bought her a big glass of lime juice to restore her strength and spirit.

Under the circumstances it was not surprising that the last extras went on hatless, some without walking sticks, others minus hair ribbons—but they were put very far back from the camera.

JENNY BEAVAN (COSTUME DESIGNER)

*O*NE OF THE JOYS *of working with Italians is that they are so terribly vain. They always made sure they looked good all day long, and that saved us an enormous amount of work. It was enchanting to watch the men strut around in perfect period dress adjusting each others' bow ties—unlike the chaotic English who had to be straightened out all the time and still managed to look a mess.*

Even though my chief memory of making A Room with a View *is of masses of costume fittings all day—refitting, altering, rushing to and from the set, washing, ironing, cleaning up the mess, and chronic fatigue—I remember it as being a very happy time, which is all the more strange when I consider the problems we had.*

Each day there was a huge amount of washing to be done, and I had arranged to have a washing machine brought over on the costume truck from England. John Bright, my co-designer, has always been terribly opposed to using washing machines and insists that everything at his company, Cosprop, be washed by hand. Here, I thought, was a perfect opportunity to rid him of this prejudice, and in doing so perhaps make life a little easier on those who labored in the Cosprop laundry. So, when the machine arrived, I decided to give John a demonstration of the efficiency and time-saving qualities of this device. I filled it up, put the shirts in, turned it on, proudly stood back—and watched in silent horror as the thing flooded all over the ancient stone floor. "Yes. Exactly. And that is why we don't use washing machines," said John calmly, managing to look both superior and smug even while he stood ankle-deep in soapy water.

Somewhere in the background Ismail was giving almost nightly dinner parties. I only managed to get to one, and that was on a night Ismail had cooked a meal exclusively carnivorous apart from the omnipresent rice. As I don't eat meat, it was the only

The restaurant Il Cavallino

Opposite:
Interior of the café Gilli

*time in our long friendship that I left one of Ismail's famous dinners even more raven-
ous than when I arrived.*

$\mathcal{A}$s if all the dramas of that morning weren't
enough to cope with, I also had to play host to Mayor Lando Conti, whom we had
invited to the piazza to watch the first day of shooting and then join us for lunch.
He regretted that he was too busy to come to the set—but lunch, of course, was
another matter. Peter Marangoni recommended a restaurant called Il Cavallino,
right on the corner of the piazza and Via delle Farine, which leads into it. In other
places, the quality of restaurants in tourist areas is usually poor, but Peter assured
me that very few restaurants in Florence make concessions to the tourist trade. In
any case, Il Cavallino was one of the most highly regarded restaurants in Florence
and had been in the hands of the same family since it opened in 1945. It was also,
as we were about to discover, one of the mayor's favorite places.

Dealing with the adventures of the Piazza—the extras and demonstrators,
cranes, pigeons, people, costumes, and traffic—made me late for lunch, and by the
time I arrived at the restaurant the mayor was already halfway through a plate of
pasta and looking very much at home. He explained that he frequently ate at Cavallino, and they always dished up his pasta as soon as they saw him walking through
the door. The mayor suggested I should try one of the restaurant's specialities,
Agnello alla Cavallino con Patate. Roast lamb and potatoes may not sound all that
special, but Italian menus don't go in for flowery details: the prosaic title of the
dish couldn't even begin to do justice to the tender thigh of lamb stuffed with rosemary, sage, and garlic, served with the tiniest and most perfect roast potatoes. I
had never come across such an aromatic stuffing and the lamb was the sweetest
and tenderest I had ever eaten.

My curiosity about this dish soon launched us onto the subject of food again.
The mayor confirmed what I had begun to suspect: that it is the combination of
the region's geographical position, climate, and most of all, a soil so rich and fer-
tile that everything that grows on it or feeds on it has an unusually full and mellow
taste. This explains why, although one can cook Tuscan recipes anywhere, the
results can never taste the same as they do in Tuscany.

Once the mayor and I began discussing food, every other concern became
irrelevant, and with so much to say about the varieties of meat sauce for pasta, I

completely forgot about the shooting, the crowds and everything else outside in the piazza, and he doubtfully put managing Florence out of his mind as well.

Surprisingly, only very few restaurants in Italy serve coffee on the premises. There is a formal ritual to the postprandial coffee, and one soon gets into the habit of the *passeggiata*—the short stroll for the purpose of digestion—to a favorite café. There, one has the choice of a café normale (the straight espresso), a café lungo (a weaker espresso), a macchiato (with the merest splash of milk), or a corretto (with a more generous splash of brandy or other liqueur). After the coffee perhaps a drink, and sometime after that an ice cream or sorbetto. And thus one can use up an entire afternoon or evening in a wholly delightful manner.

Florence is full of cafés, and we visited most of them, but I kept coming back to Gilli in the Piazza della Repubblica. It originated as a bread shop about two hundred fifty years ago and moved into the present premises in 1910—two years after Forster published *A Room with a View*. The handsome Edwardian interior is unchanged from that time, and perhaps it was that association which drew some of us there: polished wood paneling on the walls, lofty arches, gleaming brass, bargello tapestry chairs, and a rather formal atmosphere. In summer most people choose to sit at one of the umbrella-shaded tables outside, but I always preferred to sit inside in order to admire the perfect elegance of the surroundings.

While we were shooting in Florence I had news from home that two of my nieces, Sadhya and Arshi, were coming to Italy from India as part of a school trip to Europe, and Pisa, with its famous Leaning Tower, would be one of their stops. I wanted to see the girls, so Dick Robbins and I drove to Pisa early in the morning to collect them and bring them to Florence for the day. In the car they collapsed from fatigue and the time change—Bombay is four and a half hours ahead of Italy—and I thought a visit to Gilli would revive and amuse them. The sight of all the varieties of pastries and cakes brought the girls back to life and they became very animated. Thus fortified, we took them all around Florence, and afterwards, exhausted, they slept all the way back to Pisa.

For me, this day was an unexpected and refreshing interlude from the routine of organizing and shooting a film. We had flown into and out of Pisa many times on our way to Florence but always in such a hurry that we had never gone into the city. This time we went as tourists, and we dutifully climbed the two hundred ninety-four steps all the way to the top of the Campanile.

Exertion of that kind justifies the extravagance of the best ice cream in Flo-

~

Vegetables on display in the stalls

Produce destined for the market stalls

rence, so when Dick and I returned we went straight to Vivoli, acknowledged throughout Italy as one of the great ice-cream makers. Vivoli had become the unit's vice, and at any time of the day some or other of the unit would be there. People would vanish mysteriously from the set and return a little while later wiping away from their chins and noses the sticky evidence of debauch.

*I*T WAS TOWARD the end of the second week of shooting that I began to notice a certain restlessness in the unit. Those who knew me well started to drop hints; they told me of a place in Florence that sold ginger, they asked me if it was possible to make pellau with Italian arborio rice or was it essential to use Indian basmati rice for the dish? They wanted to know if I was fasting because of Ramadan. In other words, they were anticipating a curry party. The curry party has now become a tradition on Merchant Ivory films and those who had worked with me before were expecting it almost as a condition of their employment. The newcomers had heard so much about "Ismail's curry parties," they were keen to discover what all the fuss was about.

To throw a curry party I need only one thing—a very, very good friend who will allow me access to her kitchen. So I went to see Elizabeth Marangoni, who had already played a small part in the film, that of one of the Pensione Bertolini regulars, Miss Pole. She hadn't been daunted by the cameras, and I hoped she wouldn't be daunted by a curry party with seventy guests.

We chose the end of that week, Friday, May 17. Early that morning I went down to the Mercato Sant'Ambrogio in the Piazza Ghiberti to buy the food. I love street markets and had already visited all the ones in Florence many times. Florence's most famous market is the Mercato Centrale at San Lorenzo, only a few dozen yards from the church of San Lorenzo where a street market has existed since the third century. The food market now occupies an impressive double-story Art Nouveau glass and iron structure. Inside the huge space, stalls are laid out like a series of still-life paintings—each stall-holder apparently an artist manqué, artfully arranging the vibrantly colored produce to the maximum advantage. This is both a wholesale and retail center, so trading begins early—first, the chefs from the city's restaurants come to make their selection from the enormous variety offered, then the ordinary shoppers arrive.

Although Italians do have refrigerators and freezers, they still prefer to buy their food fresh and use it immediately. So visiting the market is a daily (and sometimes twice-daily) routine, and the marketplaces buzz all day until suppertime—just as they do in India, though there it is a necessity because households with refrigeration are less common than in the West.

Of all the street markets in Florence, Sant'Ambrogio was the one I liked best. It was just the right size; neither so small that it was limited in variety, nor so large that it was confusing and tiring. A central covered space encloses the stalls for meat, fish, cheese, and dairy products, and the surrounding pavements outside are lined with stalls of fresh vegetables, fruit, and flowers.

The street markets in Florence have much in common with the open markets of India, and in particular, I was reminded of Crawford Market, the largest and finest in Bombay. In both cities the stall-holders take pride in the excellence of their produce and go to great lengths to compose visually pleasing displays.

Another significant similarity between the food cultures of India and Italy is in the importance of vegetables. The majority of Indians are Hindu and, therefore, vegetarian; so vegetables, along with rice and pulses, are the staple diet throughout India. Because vegetables play such an important role in the Indian diet, they are prepared with great care and imagination. I discovered that Italians, too, regard vegetables as a principal part of their cuisine rather than just an accompaniment to meat and fish. Vegetables are usually served as an individual course during a meal and, even when they are used as an adjunct, they are always served on a separate plate.

In Italy, as in India, the variety of vegetables is so abundant and the methods of cooking them so varied that, in summer, meals frequently consist of nothing more than pasta and fresh vegetables, prepared in dozens of different and delicious ways. Wild mushrooms, for example, are plentiful and popular in Italy, and during the mushroom season it is not unusual for restaurants to offer all three courses—antipasto, primo piatto, and secondo piatto—composed only of different varieties of mushrooms cooked in appropriate ways. The eggplant is another of the many vegetables substantial enough for a main course and adaptable enough to lend itself to a number of ways of being cooked.

However, whereas the Indian climate allows most vegetables to be grown year round, Tuscan cooking is seasonal, and May is the time of the *primizie*—the spring vegetables: asparagus, endive, chard, fennel, artichokes, early green beans, and best of all, the sensational garden peas and the tiny aromatic *fragole del bosco*, wild strawberries so delicate they seem to dissolve on contact with the mouth. All the produce is grown locally and brought to the market within hours of being harvested, and sold while still shedding its Tuscan soil. There is no processing, no packaging, no grading—no interference of any kind. A bean picked at dawn will be sold in the market before noon and cooked by suppertime.

It is impossible to pass a stall without hearing the gentle imperative *saggi*—taste it, or *provi*—try it. The stall-holders will offer you a handful of this, or a bunch of that as you pass by. They know what they're doing—one taste and you buy a kilo of this, a crate of that. They encourage you to touch, to smell, to taste; they inquire about what you will make with the beans or the zucchini and advise you to choose this variety rather than another because it better suits that particular dish; and, as you leave, they wish you *buon appetito*.

Choosing the food is part of the fun of cooking, and the Italians understand this. In England and America you are often forbidden to touch the produce, and stall-holders shout and wave their arms angrily at anyone who disobeys this law.

What I cook for a dinner party depends on what is available at the market, and I usually try to use whatever local ingredients will combine well with the basic spices of Indian cooking. Inside the market there was a stall covered entirely with sardines so fresh you could still smell the sea on them. I bought them all, and then found some dill to make a dill sauce for the fish. Of course there would be rice and dal and, finally, one Italian dish. So I bought some cannelloni to stuff with a meat sauce that would be rather more exotic than the traditional one. I usually serve fresh fruit for dessert, but on this occasion the tempting glazed fruit tarts at Gilli's, glistening like Fabergé works of art, were irresistible.

Until I returned with my boxes and bags and packages, I don't think Elizabeth had really visualized quite how much food was involved in the dinner we were planning. We stood in her kitchen knee-deep in carrier bags and baskets, parcels spilling out their contents over the heaped table. What alarmed Elizabeth even more than this invasion of food was the fact that I was going back to the set and that I was not planning to return until about an hour before the arrival of the guests. I tried to reassure her that one hour was ample time for the preparation of the food, but she looked doubtful. She probably imagined I would be late and that she would have to cope with seventy hungry and expectant people and a lot of raw fish. I returned,

as good as my word, at eight o'clock and went straight to work in her kitchen.

By the time the guests began to arrive, the smell of Indian spices had floated out of the stone windows of the villa and hung over the courtyard where everyone assembled. Some came straight from shooting, others had had time to dress up—it was the usual motley but happy assembly of colleagues and friends eating and relaxing together after the day's wrap. The food had been laid out in Elizabeth's dining room, and people quickly made their way there and began trying all the various dishes.

The party was such a success that no one wanted to leave and, as a host, naturally nothing pleases me more than seeing my guests having fun and enjoying my food. But the following day was a working one with a six A.M. call, and I was anxious, in a way, to see them leave—especially the actors and the makeup artists and hairdressers who must always be the first ones on the set in order to get ready.

When everyone had finally and reluctantly left, the Marangonis, their servants, and I cleared away the debris and washed up between toasts of grappa.

A week later, to mark the last day of shooting at the Villa Maiano, I organized another party for the crew and this time, in honor of Italy, I cooked only pasta. The Italians have many versions of the traditional bolognese sauce but I made a very different kind—one completely unknown to them. A good bolognese is something the Italians are very fussy about, so I was interested to see how they would take to a sauce that, in addition to the usual ingredients, had green chillies and ginger in it. It both surpassed their expectations and pleased them, and caused some explosions not only in their mouths but in their heads. But they kept coming back for more, and halfway through the evening I had to return to the kitchen and boil some more penne so that we could finish up all the sauce.

The Florentine idyll was nearly over. Filming would continue in England, of course, at the house of my very dear friend John Pym, and we were all looking forward to that. But I would miss Florence.

There were three important scenes left to shoot—two scenes "with a view," and the film's opening shot of the disappointed Charlotte Bartlett and Lucy Honeychurch staring out of the window of their room with no view.

Rooms without views, as we had already discovered, were plentiful, and we finally chose one that was practically on our doorstep. Earlier on, Virginia Marasco had recommended we should eat at the Buca dell'Orafo, a small restaurant quite literally around the corner from the Quisisana in the parallel street. We went there often, both because its location was convenient and because the food was excellent; it had practically become our canteen. The street is scarcely more than an alley, and the buildings on either side of it connect in places above street level to form something like an arcade. It was the gloomy shuttered window of a Quisisana back bedroom that looked into this dark alley that became Lucy and Charlotte's room with no view.

The terrace above the Oltrarno, which Gianni Quaranta had now ingeniously transformed into a room, was the setting for the last remaining Florentine scenes still to be shot: Lucy Honeychurch throwing open the shutters of the room she got through exchange onto her spectacular view for the first time; and Lucy and George Emerson, the two lovers finally united in the film's last scene, embracing in silhouette against the landmarks of the city that had brought them together.

Whatever problems we had encountered while shooting in the Piazza Signoria and Santa Croce were nothing compared with the near havoc the city was about to wreak on us now—or was it the other way around? In order to make sure no modern cars were in the long shots of the city center seen to such advantage in our view, we had to stop the traffic—and in doing so we brought practically the whole of Florence to a standstill.

The Arno, with its famous bridges, divides the historic part of the city into two halves. Like Paris, with its traffic hurtling along both banks of the Seine, Florence uses its riverbanks in the same way. We chose to shoot in the late afternoon, as the last sun was fading on the monuments—in other words, at rush hour.

As usual, we were understaffed, with a handful of Italian-speaking assistants, when we needed an army of them. I would have to help. I stationed myself out of sight with our Italian assistants and a very sympathetic Italian female police officer who had been assigned to us. Neither of us spoke the other's language, but we understood each other's sign language and managed to communicate perfectly. We had devised a system of white flags: when shooting was to begin on the terrace, the crew would wave white flags to indicate that we had to stop the traffic, and when that was achieved, I waved white flags to let them know they could shoot. They would signal again when the shot was over and I would let the traffic through. But not for long—only a few cars at a time.

Gradually there was gridlock all the way to the other side of the city: cars and

The raw material for a meal at the Marangoni's

Opposite:
Flowers and fruit in the Marangoni courtyard

trucks were jammed on the bridges and far beyond. The motorists cursed this apparently crazy figure dressed in a kurta and pyjama who was waving white flags in the air, and honked their horns and revved up their scooters at me.

As well as regulating the cars, we also had to keep the pedestrians out of shot. Dusk is the preferred shopping time in the summer in Italy, so the streets were full. At one point when I saw a figure creeping out from a rather grand leather shop behind us, I pushed it back into the shop and yelled "Get down and stay down." When the shot was over, I saw the figure tentatively peering out of the shop again and realized it was Maggie Smith. I rushed in to her to apologize. "Darling," she drawled in her inimitable way, "don't worry. But you look so *demented*."

*J*UST BEFORE the end of our Italian shoot the wives and families of the Italian crew came to Florence, staying outside the city beyond Fiesole, and one night they invited me to join them for dinner in a restaurant nearby. With so much to do at the end of the shoot, I was delayed and got to the restaurant late, after everyone had begun eating. When I arrived, a plate of veal cooked with capers in some kind of nutty sauce, which was incredible, was put in front of me. But what I enjoyed more than the delicious food was the atmosphere the Italian crew generated—they were all so friendly and happy it was truly like being part of a huge family. There were arguments and discussions and shouting, and everyone hugged and kissed each other, and even people I'd never met before were hugging and kissing me. It was a happy night.

Elizabeth Marangoni became our hostess-victim for the last time when she agreed to let us use her house again for the wrap party—the traditional gala event that marks the end of shooting. This party was for everyone—for the cast and crew, for the townspeople and officials who had helped, and for all the people we had met as strangers and who had now become our friends. It was a perfect summer night, and we ate outside on Elizabeth's glorious terrace—shrimp with a dressing of olive oil and mustard, beef baked with garlic and ginger, and a huge pellau of rice.

At the end of the evening the Italian crew gave me an unexpected gift. In twenty-five years of filmmaking I had never before, except in India, been given a present by a foreign crew, and I was touched by the affection of these Italians. Inside the package was a very fine silver frame in the shape of a horseshoe—for luck, they said. But it was the inscription that was most touching—*Per il produttore più simpatico*—for the most congenial producer. They told me they would never forget me. And I would not forget them.

There were no emotional farewells that night because I knew that someday I would come back. I didn't know when: life calls you to other commitments, to other work. But the links I had established with Florence were permanent and wouldn't be broken by distance or time. *Ci vedremo* we said—we shall see each other again.

$\mathcal{A}$ ROOM WITH A VIEW was to become our most successful film and one of the most popular films of 1986. Florence had affected our professional lives and was also responsible for some dramatic changes in my kitchen. In the past I had often cooked pasta when I wanted to prepare a simple meal for unexpected guests, but I had never been very adventurous about it. I really wasn't aware of its possibilities. We do not cook with pasta at all in India except for a very special feast-day pudding made with vermicelli, pistachios, almonds, cream, and milk. The only dishes which bear any similarity to Italian food are *kedgeree,* made from rice, lentils, cloves, and chicken stock, which in texture should be very mushy, rather like a good risotto, and *keema,* the Indian stew of minced beef, tomatoes, onions, and spices, which seems to have an affinity with a bolognese sauce.

Nevertheless, it was in India that I tasted pasta for the first time. It was at one of the old British-style clubs in Bombay that assume cosmopolitan status by offering an "international" menu. So my very first experience of Italian food was spaghetti, which, in this particular establishment, came served with tomatoes and baked beans.

When I moved to New York and was living near Washington Square, I ate pasta all the time in one or another of the Italian restaurants in Greenwich Village. In those days in New York there seemed to be only three kinds of pasta sauce: bolognese, ladled on by the cupful; vongole, often from canned clams; and a not very tasty Alfredo, tending to gumminess. These were standard. The proliferation of restaurants offering so-called North Italian cuisine was a decade away.

But after my visits to Florence, in order to make *A Room with a View,* pasta

A market stall in Florence with a "decorated" scale

Below:
Ismail Merchant succumbing to the plea "provi, provi"

Opposite:
Fruit at the market

became a staple in my kitchen. It is fast and easy to cook, very nutritious, and more flexible than almost any other food. At its most simple it can be served just with a dressing of the best olive oil and, perhaps, some cheese, or it can be accompanied by dozens of different kinds of sauces. I knew I could never achieve the taste of Tuscany, either in New York or London, but I could hope to capture its spirit.

ELIZABETH MARANGONI

*S*OME OF THE *happiest memories we have of those two months were the evenings at our villa when Ismail would ask permission to cook dinner for whoever of the cast and technicians wanted to get together.*

Even though he had been working with his usual astonishing energy for at least ten hours, he would rush into the house, full of enthusiasm and anticipating the happy evening ahead. With him were always two young volunteers from among the technicians, all laden with bags of the necessary ingredients for Ismail's specialities. Down came all the pots and pans and out spilled the lentils and the rice and various vegetables and spices. We were always twenty or twenty-five people, and I was a happy guest in my own house.

(1985)

Six years later we were again the honored and happy hosts to Ismail and four of his Room with a View *team, who were to re-create through photos and recipes the many wonderful places where we ate as well as what we ate during the period of filming. The result was, of course, hours of wandering among the outdoor markets and side streets and small squares. We wound a slow way among the stalls of the Sant' Ambrogio market square, exclaiming and pricing the really beautiful displays of brilliant flowers, tomatoes, cherries, peppers, eggplant, ropes of garlic, and baskets of figs. The masses of color gleaming in the sun plus the variety of faces of the local shoppers and the country vendors were worthy of a Fellini (or a Merchant Ivory) film.*

Ismail gave us a memorable dinner party out on the terrace, away from the extreme heat of the city and with, instead, the Tuscan countryside to contemplate. Our company was reduced, but the enjoyment remained the same.

(1991)

*I*T HAS LONG been my habit to disregard conventional combinations of ingredients and freely adapt "classical" recipes in my own way. Italian cuisine is ideal for this technique because the origins of Italian food are rooted in peasant culture: this means cooking with whatever is in season, whatever is available, whatever there is a glut of, or whatever is left over from yesterday. Consequently, the cook has to be both resourceful and imaginative. There are no hard and fast rules, and as the cuisine is regional as well as seasonal, the varieties of any one dish are endless. The basic tomato sauce of the north of Italy, for example, is quite different from that of the south. So each region, each family practically, has a version of its own—not unlike the many varieties of Indian dishes lumped under the name of "curry."

All my enjoyment of cooking comes from creating and inventing, which is why I have no interest at all in exactly following classic recipes. There is a great skill, of course, in being able to make a faultless terrine de ris de veau or a soufflé d'ecrevisses; but much as I might enjoy eating a perfect canard à l'orange, if I were to make it, I would probably substitute some other wild fowl or try it with pink grapefruit instead of orange, just to see how it tasted that way. My curiosity about food makes me incapable of following orders. That could be a flaw, or it might on some occasions be a blessing.

So, I experiment. In this case I imposed Indian influences on Italian cuisine and vice versa. This kind of cooking enlarges and expands the options of a cook, and so one should never be afraid of being too experimental or too bold.

But I have to admit that, though unaware of it at the time, I was, surprisingly, not the first to unite the cuisines of Italy and India. Subsequently, I discovered that this cross-pollination had already occurred in the Middle Ages. Archives show that the great Italian explorers, as far back as Marco Polo, had returned to Italy from their Eastern travels bearing cargoes of oriental spices. Venice, then the greatest trading center in Europe, was the first Western city to discover the taste of spiced food. Rare and expensive, spices were restricted to the tables of the court, the aristocracy, and the merchant classes and, therefore, never widely influenced Italian cuisine. But, even today, and especially in the south of the country, one sometimes comes across uncharacteristic and spicy dishes whose origins clearly date back to these times. In Venice, for example, there still exists a dish of duck cooked with a prodigious amount of ginger, which has descended from these

Ismail captures his prey...

...and prepares to cook it.

Opposite:
The ingredients of the "good, honest,
and simple" Tuscan fare

medieval times. Basil, the predominant herb of Italian cooking, originated in India and Persia and, though hardly used in Indian cooking, has for many centuries had an inextricable association with Italian cuisine.

For me, the starting point is always the discovery of ingredients with which I am not familiar. And because they are a novelty, I am not intimidated by them; I have no idea of what is not possible. In Italy I discovered basil, rosemary, capers, and olives, none of which we use in India. But more than any single ingredient it was pesto that most inspired me. This pungent sauce made from basil leaves, pine nuts, parmesan cheese and olive oil is traditionally used only on pasta, but I found that it can be used very successfully on practically everything. I use it with chicken, fish, vegetables—especially on green string beans and potatoes—sometimes neat, sometimes diluted with vinegar and grated ginger, which makes it even more interesting, and occasionally mixed with grated cheese, but more often, not. A spoonful of pesto in homemade mayonnaise gives it a sensational and very different taste.

Similarly, I have added red or green chillies, or grated ginger, to basic tomato sauce which really adds zing, and I have invented sauces for pasta that incorporate ginger, mint, coriander, caraway seeds and cumin. Vice-versa, I now add dried Italian herbs like basil, oregano, and fennel to tandoori chicken, for example. And it all works because good cooking isn't about whether you get something right or wrong but creating a fine meal that everyone enjoys.

The absence in Florence of nouvelle cuisine was a relief to me: I have never been able to see the point of presenting food as a visual art in such a deliberate and labored manner. Italians have too much respect for their food to torture it in the way that particular fashion dictates, as well as heartier appetites. I shall never forget a restaurant in London that served a dish of three different kinds of filleted fish—neatly plaited together. Had the dish been worthy of comment I wouldn't have known whether to send my compliments to the chef or the coiffeur.

Italian food is good, honest, and simple, and the meal still plays an important part in the daily lives of the people. The Italian playwright Eduardo de Filippo wrote a whole play about a ragu. It was a little more than that, of course, but, finally, the preparation and the consummation of the ragu is the heart of *Saturday, Sunday, Monday*. When Franco Zeffirelli (a Florentine) staged this play at the Old Vic in the early seventies, he insisted that Joan Plowright should actually cook the ragu on stage so that the audience would understand its importance and its significance to Italian family life.

This attitude, that food is one of the pleasures central to life, also governs the way restaurants operate in Italy. Most of them are almost an extension of the family dining room. The atmosphere is relaxed and there is none of the artifice and formality so many restaurants assume because they believe the customer will be impressed.

I do sometimes enjoy the lofty ambience of grand restaurants such as those of Paris, like Le Grand Vefour and Maxim's, but that is part of their tradition and it suits them. You go there partly for the splendid show. But in lesser kinds of restaurants, the "ambience" can come off as simply pompous, pretentious, and ridiculous; you may feel you're paying for that, and not for the food and service.

In Florence it never mattered whether we were all dressed up like proper Signori and Signorine, or whether we arrived crumpled and tired, straight from shooting. Whatever our condition, the patron saw it as a duty to make us feel comfortable and happy, which was done without fuss, without tiresome ritual, and without fail. In addition to that, Florence is the only city in my experience where a restaurant guide is superfluous because every restaurant seems to be able to produce memorable meals.

Food aside, I think one of the reasons I was so drawn to Florentine restaurants was because they appear to be governed by the same principles by which we make our films. It is always said of Merchant Ivory films that all the money is on the screen: that is, it goes into the production values rather than on glamorous living off set. In much the same way, Florentine restaurants put all the cost of the meal into the food. The decor is usually very simple, often nonexistent in fact; there are no formidable armies of chefs and sous-chefs, no starched, choreographed waiters (often the patron is the waiter or the chef, and sometimes both), and no high-tech gadgetry to confuse the skill, palette, and art of the cook. Indeed, the kitchen of Coco Lezzone measures about five feet by twelve feet and most of that space is taken up by a wood-burning stove on which they cook the famous Florentine steak.

JAMES IVORY (DIRECTOR)

*O*FTEN JOURNALISTS *have asked me the question, "Why E. M. Forster?" But after making three of his novels into films, all well received and widely seen, I think their success with the public is itself justification for adapting that much-read author's work. However, in the case of* A Room with a View, *there was*

The director, James Ivory, preparing a shot

another reason beyond Forster's special qualities that attracted me as a filmmaker, a reason neither literary nor cinematic. Forster's third book afforded me an opportunity to return to Italy, a country where I had once been very happy making a film—my first—when I was young, and to which I had not gone for more than twenty years because I was too busy elsewhere. The journalists catch on at once when I mention this pragmatic reason for wanting to make A Room with a View and sigh, "Oh, yes! Italian food is so wonderful!"—as if it had mainly been food that brought me back to Italy after such a long absence. But as this is a book that celebrates Italian food, it would not be out of place to go along to some extent with that idea. I cannot deny that when the morning plane bringing me from London was about to land at the Pisa airport, I was much looking forward to my first Italian lunch in two decades, and hoping I would not be too late for it. Our friend Peter Marangoni, who features a lot in this book, was at the airport to meet me, and we left at once by road for Lucca, on the way to Florence, my final destination.

Peter was also looking forward to a good lunch, and we drove very fast up the steep and twisting road toward the mountain pass and away from the sea in the direction of Lucca. He knew exactly what restaurant there we would go to, and was counting on the chef not closing his kitchen too early. When we arrived I was told to bring my bags inside so they would not be stolen out of the back of the car. The restaurant adjoined the tall jumbled oval of tenements and palazzi built on top of the ruins of the old Roman amphitheater, and I regret I cannot remember its name, but it was classic in every way, and the perfect place for such a celebratory meal. It was welcoming, yet dignified; somewhat expensive, but not too much so; the food was wholesome, yet refined; the ingredients were the freshest, but the recipes ancient.

What is the main visual impression one gets from the typical, respectable restaurant of this kind in Italy? For me, it is how much white there is everywhere. The white starts at the floor, which is often tiled with the little hexagonal tiles American builders used in kitchens and bathrooms at the turn of the century, that can easily be mopped clean; then, the yards of white cloth on the tables and up the fronts of the waiters, and over the laps of the diners, or tucked under their chins; the china, invariably white, too, and even the pasta in it, still white and not smothered under masses of red sauce as in America; and the broken rolls of delicious white bread that you spread with white, unsalted butter.

White, and creamy light colors, everywhere—in contrast to the black clothes of the waiters, who animate the scene as they energetically rush about, making it resemble an Impressionist or Postimpressionist painting or print. I have known these waiters to suddenly sit down at the corner of one's table to figure the bill and rest their feet. No one seems put off by that in Italy, which strikes me as being the most democratic country in Europe.

*T*HIS LACK of gadgetry was another blessing. From the Porta al Prato to the Porta Romana I never saw, either in a restaurant or in a private kitchen, a single microwave. Who needs gadgets when there is so much skill and passion in the kitchen? Some of my happiest moments were those I spent cooking in the company of Florentines, themselves skilled cooks: poised over a stove like two musicians about to perform a duet, taking our cues from each other, responding to each others' variations with ever more surprising phrases, momentum increasing with the rising heat as the complex virtuoso displays grew bolder, more inventive, surging to a steamy crescendo—appoggiaturas and fiorituras flying around all over the kitchen.

I learned a great deal from the Italians, and I feel I gave them something in exchange. As a daring amateur—which is what I consider myself in the kitchen—I was delighted when those epicurean masters asked me for my recipes. They received my adaptations of familiar Italian dishes enthusiastically, and accepted them without reservations: they may be purists in matters of quality, simplicity and taste, but never pedantic about how good results are achieved. Italian cuisine isn't about the right way or the wrong way of cooking, but about different ways.

*S*OME YEARS AGO I had the idea of writing about all the cities where I had worked and, as a consequence, cooked. Proposals were drawn up, contracts were signed and, as I went off to make more films, deadlines for the book came and went. I thought the publishers might have forgotten all about it, but at the end of 1990 I received a polite letter asking when they might expect to receive my manuscript. My original idea had been to incorporate Florence, Paris, London, New York, Los Angeles, and Bombay in one volume, but the

Dinner at Coco Lezzone

more I thought about it, the clearer it seemed that one book alone could not do justice to all these places: each city merited its own account. The publishers agreed to the new, expanded, and more ambitious plan, and I began to think about Florence very seriously, even though in terms of my filmmaking career, it is out of chronological order. I chose to start with Florence because of the deep impression it had made on me and all the happy memories associated with that city. I had always intended to return, but other commitments had intervened; I never imagined it would be six years before I would be able to go back there.

It was an odd coincidence that this came about at the time we were preparing to shoot *Howards End*—the film Ruth had always championed and that had, in a way, because of her enthusiasm for E. M. Forster, set in motion the making of *A Room with a View.*

The trip to Florence was planned to take place as soon as the shooting of *Howards End* finished in early July, and I telephoned Elizabeth Marangoni to ask her if she minded having guests. This threat had been hanging over her ever since the book was first planned, and whenever we met or corresponded, I promised her it would happen soon: but things would come up and the trip kept being postponed. So she received the latest news bulletin with both enthusiasm and trepidation. By coincidence her son, Peter, who was busy designing and building a house in Turkey, was also going to be in Florence at the same time, so it would be a real reunion, though, disappointingly, it would lack Jim, who had to return to America to begin editing *Howards End.*

$\mathcal{B}$ESIDES MYSELF our party was made up of Dick Robbins, Helena Bonham Carter, Anna Kythreotis, a Greek friend and writer, and Derrick Santini, the stills photographer of our last two films, to take the pictures for the book.

We were on the early Alitalia flight to Pisa and had to rise in a gray London dawn to get to the airport on time. The flight was delayed, but when we eventually emerged out of the plane into the shimmering heat-haze of the Pisa airport and saw the blue sky and breathed the heady Tuscan air, we felt joy at returning to a place where we had been so happy. The train to Florence was about to leave the station and there was a long queue at the ticket office. We just wanted to get to the city without any more delays, so we ran for the train—even though there is a double charge for tickets bought on board. We rushed down the concourse with our bags flying and caught the train just as it was pulling out of the station. After thirty years in the business, I still haven't managed to assume the archetypal image of the film producer. We will always be itinerant gypsies—it's a lot more fun.

As the train made its way to Florence, we feasted on the glorious summer landscape. Bare fields were transformed into a canvas of brilliant sunflowers nodding lazily, gold as far as the eye could see; the grapevines were clothed in dense, lush green foliage, and everywhere the blood-red lakes of the tomato crops.

The party returns: Helena Bonham Carter, Anna Kythreotis, Peter Marangoni, Ismail Merchant, and Richard Robbins

Even the olive groves were flourishing again. On our last visit to Florence there had been a great deal of concern that the freak storms of the preceding cold and wet winter had destroyed the groves. But the Greeks believe that the olive tree never dies, and no matter how the tree may be destroyed above the surface the roots will always survive and sprout again.

Peter came to the station to meet us, and then we piled into two cars and drove off toward Arcetri. Helena and Dick were to stay at the house of Helena's grandmother, Propper de Callejon, on a hilltop near the slope covered with the reviving olive trees where the Marangoni villa stood. So we dropped them off and continued down the road to Elizabeth's house.

The Marangoni terrace was now a jungle of geraniums; they grew out of the ground, along the parapets, in every nook and broken brick. Wherever one looked there were geraniums in every color and variety. In the past Elizabeth had often expressed regret that I wasn't seeing the garden at its best, and now I understood why. She came out to greet us, and from that time, whenever I think of Elizabeth, I always picture her framed by her geraniums.

The courtyard inside was even more astonishing: not just geraniums but seemingly every other kind of flower, and a four-foot-high gardenia bush laden with

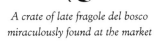

A crate of late fragole del bosco
miraculously found at the market

waxy white blossoms that filled the whole courtyard with their pungent sweet smell.

As we had only five days to accomplish everything, Peter had wanted to know what our plans were so that he could organize the maximum of activity in that time. That night he had arranged for us to have dinner at Coco Lezzone. Franco Paoli, the patron, greeted us enthusiastically, and as soon as we had sat down he brought us baskets of casalinga—the plain, crusty, home-made Tuscan bread— because he remembered that it was my favorite. It was so pleasant to sit among friends, enjoying an easy, relaxed evening of good food and conversation without the conventional fuss or ritual of most restaurants one is used to. There were so many things on the menu we all wanted to try that, finally, Signore Paoli told us to leave the decisions to him and he would prepare a number of complimentary dishes that we could all share between us, and that way we could try most of the menu.

As the various dishes arrived, they were passed around, everyone trying some of this, a little of that, with murmurs of pleasure that increased with each dish. First there were tureens of pappa al pomodoro (a thick tomato and bread soup), ribollita (a soup made of vegetables, beans, and bread), zuppa di verdura (a fine vegetable soup) and minestrone freddo di riso (a cold, thick vegetable soup with rice).

Next came farfalle con porcini freschi (butterfly-shaped pasta with a sauce of fresh porcini mushrooms), rigattoni di sugo di carne (the ridged pasta with a rich meat sauce), and a huge platter of perfectly cooked canelli beans, zucchini, fagiolini beans, all dressed in olive oil and basil.

These were the appetizers. Now came the more serious part of the meal: piccatina con l'acciugata (tender veal escallopes served with anchovies), arista al forno (pork chine roasted in the oven—this is a very tender cut from the ridged part of the backbone), braciole della casa (a veal chop), and naturally, bistecca alla fiorentina—but this was the largest I had ever seen. Signore Paoli explained that it was the product of the chianina, the largest breed of cow in the world, and the only one that should be used for the traditional bistecca.

By the time we finished, the table was entirely covered with dishes, bottles, plates, and glasses, covering every last spot of the tablecloth. We stayed very late, chatting with each other, with Signore Paoli, who would join us from time to time to see how we liked the food and to finish the many, many bottles of wine that had accumulated on the table.

I slept well that night, intoxicated by the gardenia bush that insinuated its heady scent through the window, and the next morning I woke early to the sound of distant piano music—Chopin perhaps, though it was too far to tell. Elizabeth was already up and, over breakfast in the kitchen, she told me that the music I had heard was the practicing of Norberto Capelli and Hector Moreno, two Argentinian pianists who were tenants on part of her property.

The first item on our schedule that day was to go to the market at Sant'Ambrogio and buy food for the dinner party I wanted to give. It was the height of summer, and the marketplace was bursting with good things. As we made our way through the stalls, we investigated everything: glossy eggplants and colorful sweet peppers; all the various lettuces from arugula to radicchio; squash and zucchini of all shapes and sizes; fat bulbs of fennel and garlic; and every kind of fungus from the common mushroom to the rare truffle, which otherwise can only be found in France. The variety of beans alone would make a feast. Then there were the tomatoes: tiny cherry tomatoes to huge misshapen beef tomatoes and every type in between, including tomatoes still on the bush, each variety lending its own particular qualities to one dish or another. It all reminded me of the vegetables grown in Simla, in the hills of northern India.

The variety of fruit was just as vast. I counted two dozen different types of melon, and there were probably as many kinds of peaches, apricots, plums, and cherries. It was unending. Wherever we stopped to look, the stall-holders sliced into melons, split open pomegranates, broke off clusters of grapes for us to try.

We bought fruit and vegetables, then went inside and picked out fish and Florentine steak and great wedges of Parmesan cheese. Unable to carry any more, we made our way back to the car, first stopping to buy sheaves of pastel-colored campanula flowers for Elizabeth. Then we had a wonderful surprise. We stumbled on crates of fragole del bosco. The season should have been over but the storekeeper told us that, because of the bad winter, the crop was late and these were the very last. We bought a crate and picked at the strawberries all the way home.

*A*RRANGEMENTS HAD been made with Contessa Lucrezia Corsini Miari Fulcis to lunch with us at Cave di Maiano. She brought two friends with her, and also her beautiful young daughter, Chiara.

We sat outside, under canopies of sun-dappled vines making a veil of fresh, green leaves. The patron, Aldo Landi, also took charge of ordering for us and filled the enormous table with antipasti, the traditional appetite stimulants. Fresh green beans dressed with olive oil and sage; melon and prosciutto; salami and figs; pecorino—the local hard ewes' milk cheese; finocchiona—a local speciality salami made with fennel seeds.

Then, our appetites stimulated, the main courses arrived. Pappa al pomodoro again, but given a house twist, you might say; fagioli, the little haricot-type beans in olive oil; crostini al fegato, small savory toasts topped with liver pâté; a magnificent tortino di zucchini, like a flat omelette with fried zucchini on top; and an enormous bowl of farfalle al tonno e pomodoro, butterfly-shaped pasta in a tuna and tomato sauce.

There was a lot of animated chatter as we recollected the wonderful times we had during the filming at Maiano. After the shooting of *A Room with a View* I had written to the contessa to thank her for the generosity and goodwill she had shown us during the making of our film. Now she told me that she ordinarily threw letters away, but she had kept mine and one from the historian and professor of literature Piero Bargellini, who had been mayor of Florence at the time of the great flood in 1966. At that time the contessa had offered the Villa Maiano to house the people who had lost their homes. A whole camp was created in the grounds of the villa, where tents were erected all over the gardens and terraces. The mayor had written the most beautiful letter to her expressing his enormous gratitude for her assistance during that devastating period, and to that she had added the letter of thanks from a film producer, whose cast and crew had also taken over her house and garden, but for a different reason. She thought these two expressions of gratitude complemented each other—I suppose because a film company on the move is not unlike a great natural disaster, sweeping everything down before it.

The contessa told us that the previous week she had opened a gelateria up in the little town of Maiano, just a short stroll from the Cave. In the summer, people frequently drive up to the hills to escape briefly from the intense heat of the city, and the contessa thought these excursions would be even more pleasant with a place to sit and enjoy an ice cream or a cool drink. So I told the contessa about the time, many years ago, when my passion for ice cream persuaded me to open an ice-cream parlor in Manhattan. Unfortunately, my short career as an ice-cream maker came to an end when I discovered that the demands of making ice cream and making movies were totally incompatible. The image of a film producer standing behind a counter scooping out ice cream amused the contessa tremendously, and she insisted that after lunch we should go to the gelateria so that I could give her my professional opinion on the Maiano ice cream.

The Gelateria Fattoria di Maiano had been skillfully converted from a small stone farmhouse with all the original features left mostly intact. Outside, huge terrazzo umbrellas shaded the tables where we sat trying out the innumerable flavors—from fresh fruit sorbets to elaborate alcoholic ice-cream sundaes—from graceful frosted glass coupes.

After we had exhausted the repertoire of the gelateria, the contessa took us to an old convent on the estate, now converted to a center for the restoration of fine

art and textiles. It was closed for the summer months, but we wandered through the cool stone cloisters, looking into the barred windows at the antique tapestries and wall hangings in the process of being restored.

Before we left Maiano, the contessa invited us to return another day to the villa. She knew we all wanted to see it again, and she also wanted to show us around the olive press that produces the best olive oil in the region.

That evening Dick and Helena asked us to dinner at their house, the Villa San Martino, where Rosanna, the lady who looks after the house all through the year, prepared a simple meal. When we were shooting *A Room with a View,* Helena's grandmother and mother were staying at the house and one afternoon they invited me to tea. Helena's great-grandmother, Mrs. Wooster, had bought the house for a pittance in 1948 from two English ladies who panicked when it seemed that Florence would be taken over by the Communists. After a year, when the danger subsided, the English ladies tried to buy back the house, but Mrs. Wooster refused to sell. Which is how we came to be sitting on that enchanting terrace admiring yet another beautiful view—until suddenly there was an incredible downpour and we all picked up our tea-cups and rushed under the porch. There had been so much rain already that I commented on Tuscany's generosity when it comes to showering its guests with rain.

There was little chance of that happening on such a perfect summer evening. We dined outside on the jasmine-scented terrace in the glow of candlelight, surrounded by looming black cypresses. Rosanna had prepared a light, delicious meal. A tricolor salad of snowy mozzarella cheese, fresh tomato, and whole basil leaves overlaid on a huge platter like a series of miniature Italian flags. Rosanna's version of penne pomorolo, the nib-shaped pasta with tomato sauce, is a Neapolitan one with a robust, intense flavor. She had also made a refreshing salad of radicchio, endive, and wild green leaves, their bitterness bringing out even more strongly the sweetness of the olive oil in which the salad was dressed. I contributed some of the wild strawberries we had found in the market, and their appearance so late in the season was much appreciated.

This was exactly the kind of evening I most enjoy. Relaxing with close friends around a table of good food and wine, naturally we remembered all the old stories from the filming and got quite sentimental. If it was like this after the passage of only six years, what will it be like after twenty?

Peter had told Virginia and Riccardo Marasco, the owners of the Pensione Quisisana, of our visit to Florence, and they invited us for lunch at their farmhouse in Greve, right in the heart of Chianti country. This is an extensive wine-growing region and produces Italy's finest wines.

I am not a wine buff and could never become one. I can recognize and enjoy a good wine, but whether it comes from one side of the hill or the other, I cannot tell, and in any case, it is of little interest to me. Like the Italians, I feel that wine is something to be enjoyed rather than discussed and unduly fussed over. And there is certainly much to enjoy in Tuscany—from the modest Chianti Classico, to the famous Brunello di Montalcino from Siena, one of the world's great wines (and my particular favorite), to the legendary Sassicaia. The Greeks knew this country as Oenotria—the land of wine.

How important wine is to the Italians can be judged from the menu of Cave di Maiano; the list of food runs to one page, the list of wine to three. I had never been to this part of the Italian countryside before, and the hour-long drive took us deeper and deeper into wine-growing country, where every hill and valley was dense with vines.

Virginia and Riccardo were genuinely overjoyed to see us. Their three little boys were now fine young men, but Virginia and Riccardo seemed not to have changed at all. They showed us around the large farmhouse—old, rambling, and very beautiful. They showed us their chickens and ducks and invited us to pick sweetly scented and succulent apricots, cherries, and greengages from the trees in their orchard.

We sat on a tiny vine-covered, sun-stippled balcony that overlooked a dramatic valley of misty olive groves. The Marascos told us how much they appreciated our coming all that way to be with them, but I felt it was we who were privileged to be in this glorious natural landscape where everything was to be admired, where everything visually ugly and offensive was absent, and to be able to enjoy it in the company of such friends.

Virginia had prepared a traditional country lunch, with everything either grown or acquired locally. First, salami and prosciutto with melon and figs, and crostini—small savory toasts topped with a homemade piquant chicken-liver pâté. Then she served two types of pasta, one with pesto and the other with a sauce of fresh sweet peppers that I had never tried before and found so good that I begged Virginia to tell me how she made it. And, most typical of this contadino lunch, there were two kinds of insalata di campo—field or wild salad, with various green-stuff entirely unfamiliar to us: ramponcioli, bianchella, radagolio, escarole—all growing wild in these hills.

When it seemed impossible that we could eat anything more, Riccardo brought out a whole fresh ricotta cheese. This ricotta, made by a local farmer, was nothing like the travesty that goes by the name of ricotta outside Italy. It was of a soft, melting, dewy texture with a most delicate creamy taste.

In Italy, the subject of ricotta always provokes a heated debate. There are those who eat it with sugar, with honey, with preserves, with salt even. Then there are those who believe such embellishments ruin a good ricotta. But even the purists in our party were converted when Riccardo brought out a bottle of Vin Santo, the dessert wine made from semidried grapes, and drenched the ricotto with it.

Finally, Virginia had made something truly representative of Chianti—schiacciata con l'uva, a doughy pastry baked with fresh grapes and walnuts. This was accompanied with glasses of Vin Santo, the holy wine, and the combination was indeed divine.

∾

Riccardo Marasco and his chittara-lyra

Opposite:
Schiacciata bread, cheese, and wine at the house of the Marasco family at Greve

To add to the languid and relaxed mood after lunch, Riccardo brought out his chittara-lyra and serenaded us with pastoral songs.

Bella mia, questo mio core
per voi vive e per voi more
che voi siete per mia sorte
la mia vita e la mia morte.

Col bel guardo mi ferite,
col bel guardo mi guarite,
quando dunque mi mirate
morte e vita, ahimè, mi date.

O d'amor miracol novo,
vita e morte a un tempo provo
nè so qual è più gradita
se la morte oppur la vita.

Anzi in dubbio ancor io vivo
s'io son morto o s'io son vivo,
ma sia quel che vuol il fato:
vivo o morto a voi m'ho dato.

My beautiful one, this heart of mine
lives and dies for you
because you are my destiny,
my life, my death.

You wound me with your beautiful glance,
and heal me with the same,
so when you look at me
you give me life and, alas, death.

Oh new miracle of love,
I feel life and death at the same moment
but I know not which is more welcome
be it death or be it life.

Nay, still I live in doubt
whether I am dead or alive,
whatever it be that fate decrees:
alive or dead, to you I have given myself.

Sunday lunch in Italy can last all day, and well into the evening, as it might have on this occasion had not Peter reminded me at about five o'clock that I had invited twenty people, including the Marascos, to dinner at the house that night. Lost in this magical landscape and Riccardo's bucolic songs, I had forgotten all about the dinner party.

We sped back to Florence—that is, were hurled along the mountain roads in Peter's car—predicting that dinner could never be ready on time, if we arrived at all. But we did arrive, and everyone was ordered into the kitchen to start preparing the food. They had all had experience of cooking with me, so they were like a well-drilled orchestra under my baton.

Zucchini were put into one pot, potatoes and peas in another. A sauce of mustard, lemon, and rosemary was made for the mormore fish, which were cooked with mushrooms. Cloves were added to a fiery pasta sauce, and the distinctive smells of garlic, basil, cumin, and rosemary started to fill the kitchen. Salads were chopped, fruits were sliced, my sous-chefs begged for instructions, and I would add a handful of peppercorns here, a squeeze of lemon there, until all the pots were bubbling. Suddenly the guests began to arrive, and at the first sound of cars coming up the gravel drive we bolted out of the kitchen, flinging off our daytime clothes and changing hastily into something fresh. Before you could say "bistecca alla fiorentina," we had arranged ourselves against the geraniums on the terrace, the picture of composure, ready to greet our guests.

Again, we ate on the terrace, and with so many dear familiar faces around, it felt just like one of the parties we had had during the filming. We ate and chatted late into the night, and when all the guests had left, I found myself washing dish-

*The Villa Maiano transformed into the dining
room of the Pensione Bertolini*

es and pots and pans with Elizabeth, Peter, and Martino; that is a natural conclu-
sion for every chef—the process that begins in the market and ends in the small
hours at the sink, unless you are very rich, which none of us are.

*T*HE VILLA MAIANO looked exactly as I remembered
it from the first time we had gone there on our first recce in 1985. Yet somehow,
in my imagination, I had expected to see the lamps on our towers and the snaking
black cables, and our filmmaking equipment—the way it had been while we were
shooting there—as well as the small army of technicians rushing about, and trucks
moving in and out of the courtyard.

I went to the back door, as we had always done. The others stayed outside to
admire the gardens, while I entered through into the kitchen, the scene of so many
memorable moments, and called out to the contessa who had come to welcome us.

We walked into her grand reception room, which we had transformed into the

dining room of our Pensione Bertolini. It was empty and quiet: no cameras, no actors, no noise. The sun filtered through the shutters, and in the hazy half-light one could almost imagine the shadows and sounds of a scene being set up.

The ghosts pursued us into the red silk damask room where Lucy Honeychurch had played Beethoven on the piano and Reverend Beebe listened unseen. The round Victorian red seat was still in the center of the room, but there was no Reverend Beebe, no Lucy, and no piano. We walked outside onto the terrace where a hundred people once sat to eat the pasta with the explosive sauce.

The contessa had laid out a large table draped with a pink cloth for our lunch. On it, a pleasing arrangement of crystal glasses for wine and champagne. On a smaller table there was a whole pecorino—the local cheese made from goats' milk—and some schiacciata, which are flat circles of bread made with olive oil and topped with either tomatoes, zucchini, or onions.

The contessa and her daughter, Chiara, were there, and also the contessa's sister, the Marchesa Nerina Corsini Incisa della Rocchetta. They certainly are a handsome family. We drank wine from the contessa's vineyards and toasted the villa, the film, Italy, and each other. We admired the cool white wine but the marchesa told us that, although it was a very fine wine, it wasn't a patch on *hers*. Incisa della Rocchetta are the makers of Sassicaia, a wine of unfailing excellence that costs as much as Dom Perignon.

The marchesa shared my passion for cooking. She picked the wild herbs that grew in the garden and explained their uses to us. One of these was pepocino, a peppery rosemary and an optional constituent of panzanella, the summer salad of stale bread for which the marchesa gave me her own recipe. It may seem strange that a marchesa, attached to two of the oldest and noblest families of Italy, should bother about using up stale bread. "In Tuscany," she explained, "we never waste food. And Tuscan bread is made without salt, so it keeps longer and doesn't mold." Tuscan bread, even when stale, *is* too good to throw away, so it is often incorporated into soup and other recipes. Even the humblest vegetables, continued the marchesa, have a place on the Tuscan table, and she illustrated the point by telling me her mother's, the Principessa Elena Corsini, favorite way of preparing onions.

The contessa had arranged for ice cream to be brought up from her gelateria, and it arrived in a procession of four or five workers from the gelateria holding up elaborate coupes in different shapes, like an ancient procession painted on an Etruscan wall. We applauded. The ice cream had to be photographed very quickly before it melted in the sun, and when the pictures were taken, we all fell on the dazzling display like savages.

On my last departure from Florence, I had taken with me many flagons of the local Maiano olive oil, which the contessa produces. That supply had been used up long since, so the contessa took us once more to the shop on the estate that sells all the local produce. On the way we stopped at the mill where the olives are pressed and the contessa showed us around it. With over thirty thousand olive trees on her estate, the contessa is the biggest oil producer in Tuscany and the Maiano oil is the most highly regarded in the region.

Olive oil production doesn't begin until after the olives are harvested in the winter, so the mill was empty and quiet. All the oil produced here is extra virgin, that is, pure and cold pressed—the most expensive method, but it is oil of the very highest quality. At the shop we bought flagons of the oil for ourselves as well as bottles to give as gifts back home.

Before we left, the contessa gave me some solferini di montagna, rare mountain beans that are a local delicacy and, as a lentil, are a bit like wild strawberries in that they are not widely cultivated. She instructed me on how to cook them. From her sister we took with us an invitation to return to Tuscany soon with the single purpose of visiting her estate and eating at the restaurant she had recently opened there. The Sassicaia, she promised, would flow.

WE RETURNED to the Piazza Signoria to marvel once again at Neptune disporting with his nymphs and satyrs, Cosimo di Medici astride his horse, and the copy of Michelangelo's *David* that dominates this imposing space. Looking at the hundreds of people thronging there, it was difficult to imagine that we had once made these crowds vanish, swept them out of the square so we could shoot our film, after repeopling it with our own crowd, in their contrasting colors—darks for the Florentines, beiges for the northern foreigners clutching their Baedeker guide books.

Our promenade of the square brought us directly to the doorstep of Il Cavallino, where I had dined with the mayor of Florence and eaten that unforgettable lamb. After all we had eaten at the Villa that morning, no one felt like having another lunch, but we agreed it would be polite to go in and pay our respects. When the patron, Franco Martinelli, came to show us to a table I reminded him of the last occasion we had visited his restaurant, and he greeted us like long-lost friends. He insisted we should sit down there and then; there was lamb on the menu, and a wonderful antipasto of seafood, and tagliatelle served with a sauce of porcini mushrooms. Against all that, our resolve to forgo lunch couldn't stand a chance.

When the time came to leave and we asked for the bill, Signore Martinelli looked surprised and hurt. How could we think of such a thing? Our return was a cause for celebration; we had honored him, and lunch was definitely on the house. We insisted, but he remained adamant and, in the end, we had to accept gracefully. We had eaten so much that we thought it would be a good idea to walk it off with a stroll through the city. It was pleasant to walk aimlessly in the sunshine, peering into the shops and admiring the elegant displays for which Florence is so famous. Reflex led us, eventually, to the Piazza della Repubblica—and to Gilli, where we sank down in the coolness of its Edwardian halls and ordered a juice of chilled fresh apricots and iced coffee. We sniffed the scented and tinted sugars on

～

The restaurant Cave di Maiano, outdoors

Opposite:
Delights from the gelateria at the Villa di Maiano

the counter, and bought a torta della nonna, a traditional cake made from feather-light pastry and cream, to take home to Elizabeth.

We had resisted, with some difficulty, the honeyed confections inside Gilli, but outside we were ambushed by a vitrine with a dazzling display of fresh berries. Red currants, blueberries, tiny gooseberries, wild strawberries, and lampone bianco—the golden raspberries that grow locally—all tumbling voluptuously from long-stemmed glasses like gems in Bulgari's windows.

I wanted to go again to Santa Croce to light a candle in thanks for all our blessings. We arrived just as the church was closing and crowds of people were spilling out of the huge wooden doors shutting behind them. We raced up the broad steps through the crowds, and at the top were accosted by two persistent gypsy women, one of whom was carrying a tiny baby, the other a folded newspaper she was, apparently, trying to sell to me. Beggars asking for alms are a common sight at churches and shrines and I would normally give them something, but we were in a hurry.

I explained the purpose of our visit to the priest who was bolting the doors. He remembered the occasion of our filming and granted us a few minutes in the church, which was now empty but for the priests silently putting everything in order, and we felt privileged to see Santa Croce in this exclusive way.

PATRICK GODFREY (REVEREND EAGER)

I DON'T THINK *any other producer has ever been allowed to film inside Santa Croce, but somehow or other, and heaven alone knows how, Ismail persuaded both the city fathers and the Vatican, and it was agreed that we could film there from six in the morning until three in the afternoon.*

In films everything always takes longer than expected. We hadn't done even half of what we had planned before the tourists, who had been told they could come into the church at three, began thundering on the doors. Ismail, once again, used his legendary powers of persuasion and managed to get permission for us to continue shooting from six in the evening, when Santa Croce officially closed, and work through the night until we finished.

Jim suggested that Denholm Elliott and I take advantage of the three-hour pause to rehearse with the extras the scene we were to shoot next when we reconvened at six.

Actors rarely get enough rehearsal time on a film, so we immediately agreed. As an afterthought, Jim presented me with a book of Ruskin with the injunction to mug up a lecture on Santa Croce's famous Giotto frescoes as called for in the scene.

We all changed out of our costumes into normal clothes during the break and reassembled at Santa Croce, which by then was swarming with tourists. Denholm and I took up our positions in the Peruzzi chapel, and I went into my hastily prepared lecture, indicating the finer points of the frescoes to our extras who represented Edwardian tourists. I was playing a supercilious and abominably rude clergyman; Denholm was the free-thinking agnostic who contradicts my lecture. We were playing the scene for real and concentrating deeply on getting it right. I was being pompous about Giotto, Denholm was haranguing me for all he was worth, and the extras looked obligingly back and forth as per the script. But we must have been even more convincing than Jim could have hoped because we gradually became aware that we had attracted an audience.

The real tourists, who had come to gaze in awe at the Giottos, found themselves drawn instead to the periphery of our scene, startled by the unusual sight of what appeared to be a tour guide being loudly and insistently contradicted and heckled by one of his own group. We could hear the murmurs about Denholm's rudeness and his disgraceful behavior.

When Ismail realized what was going on, he was on the floor with laughter—and I noticed a gleam in his eye. Who can be sure that he wasn't seriously considering dunning the real tourists for the privilege of listening to my profoundly erudite views on thirteenth-century frescoes?

ON OUR WAY HOME we stopped off to buy some groceries, but when it came time to pay, I discovered I had been robbed. My companions were very solicitous and seemed to feel the crime more acutely than I did. The general opinion was that the gypsies were responsible, and we tried to reconstruct how it had happened. I had rushed up ahead of the others, squeezing through the oncoming exiting crowds. At the top of the steps, the two gypsies took advantage of the general crush and one tried to distract me with her crying baby, whilst the other, the newspaper folded lengthwise over her arm, emptied my pocket. In my anxiety and haste to get to the closing door I was, perhaps, less vigilant

than I should have been. Peter said he would return to the church the following day to kill the gypsies, but Dick reminded us that the gypsies had a baby, and it was possible they needed the money more than we did. I felt Dick was right, though the amount was quite large—six hundred dollars.

Whenever anything unpleasant happens to me, I try to put it out of my mind as quickly as possible. It is pointless to dwell on these kinds of misadventures and misfortunes. By the time we arrived home, I had already recovered enough to joke about not being able to eat out that night and having to make do with whatever was in the icebox.

Some of my best inventions have come about on such occasions. When I have to cook an impromptu meal, and haven't even shopped, I like to poke around in the cupboards and the refrigerator to see what is there and what can be done with it. My foraging yielded eggs, pasta, pesto, cannellini beans, and fresh yellow and green sweet peppers. So we had egg curry, pasta with salsa verde, and a salad of beans and peppers, while the gypsies dined out in splendor somewhere.

We ate on the terrace that night en famille, and Martino Marangoni brought his son, Matteo, who had just returned from summer camp and seemed delighted with this Italo/Indian supper. We finished with the torta della nonna we had bought in Gilli and made our plans for the following day. The most disagreeable aspect of the robbery was that all my cash had been taken and we would have to spend the next morning trying to find a bank that would advance cash on one of my credit cards.

We wasted the morning queuing first in one bank then another until we finally found one that was prepared to bankroll me—it was not unlike trying to raise money for a film. Dick—ever the practical Yankee—bought a money belt and took control of all the cash. But if the object of this exercise was to protect our money, Dick rather missed the point: as we discovered later in the day, he had walked all over the city with the money belt hanging open and the fat wad of notes clearly signaling "take me" to every passerby.

I announced that I would treat everyone to tripe buns, but this suggestion received a very lukewarm response from my companions. Nevertheless, we walked to the Piazza dei Cimatori where Miro Pinzauti still held court, but the tripe stall was unrecognizable. The old wooden cart had gone and in its place was a shiny new metal one under a jaunty blue and white umbrella. Signore Pinzauti assured us that the change was only cosmetic; he still prepared the tripe in the traditional way, and his tripe was the best in the whole of Italy. Certainly it tasted just as good as it always had.

Only Peter and I ate the tripe buns, so we went for lunch to Buca dell'Orafo, around the corner from the Quisisana. We arrived in the middle of the lunchtime bustle, but the patron recognized us and gave me a slap on the back by way of welcome. When he joined us to discuss what we would eat, he asked after Maggie and Denholm and Simon as though they were family. Choice defeated us completely, so we asked for a plate of almost everything and ate communally. But there was tripe on the menu, and I insisted we should have that as well, though everyone cried out that I had just had tripe on the stall.

The tripe here was as excellent as all the other dishes we tried: bracioline alla contadina (veal chops), fagioli all'uccelletto (cannellini beans stewed with tomatoes), fusilli al pomodoro fresco (pasta with a sauce of fresh tomatoes), tagliarini con piselli (pasta with a light fresh sauce of green peas), a salad of green leaves called "barba di cappuccino," which translates as "monk's beard," and, best of all, the grilled tender porcini mushrooms as large and succulent as steaks.

A lunch like that necessitated another leisurely stroll around Florence, and this time our meanderings took us to Via Isola delle Stinche where we bought ice-cream cones at Vivoli for old times' sake. We ate them as we crossed over the road to the Astra, the cinema where every summer for the past six years they have shown *A Room with a View* because, we were told, it is popular with the tourists. It seems odd that people who may well have been inspired by the film to come to Florence still wish to sit in a cinema and watch Florence on film, but it is a compliment if they do.

The next day Martino Marangoni, who is an excellent photographer, invited us to his studio in Via Zanobi to show us the striking black-and-white photographs he had taken during the shooting of A Room with a View. Afterward, he took us to a nearby restaurant, the Trattoria Mario, for lunch. Panzanella, the summer salad for which the marchesa had given me her own recipe, was on the menu, and it was a revelation. The mixture of bread, vegetables, and herbs is exactly the kind of dish that lends itself to many variations, and was something I was keen to experiment with. We also tried another new dish, lingua con salsa verde, ox tongue with an herb sauce, which was delicious. Then there was the traditional penne al ragu (nib-shaped pasta with the classic meat sauce), and a trifolato, vegetables (in this case zucchini, tomatoes and nipitella, a variety of wild mint) fried together in garlic.

Our visit to Florence came to an end. I realized that this visit was really a continuation of the last: a continuity that would be present with every future return. For, whether in six months or another six years, we would certainly return. So, once more, we avoided farewells because we would reappear in each others' lives. Once you come to know Italians, it is hard to leave them; but one never really does, for their spirit always remains to inhabit your own.

Opposite and above:
Santa Croce "without a Baedeker"

111

RECIPES

STARTERS

BRUSCHETTA

(THE ITALIAN CREW OF *A ROOM WITH A VIEW*)

24 small, thick slices of good country bread
Garlic, crushed with the blade of a knife
Olive oil
6 large, fresh ripe tomatoes, coarsely chopped
Salt and pepper

TOAST THE BREAD on both sides. Rub each slice with garlic then drizzle generously with olive oil. Mound with the tomatoes and season with salt and freshly ground pepper.   SERVES 12

CROSTINI WITH CHICKEN LIVERS

Crostini di Fegatini

(Virginia Marasco)

1 onion, finely chopped	2 tablespoons crushed capers
2 tablespoons olive oil	1 teaspoon tomato purée
6 chicken livers	Chicken stock
½ cup white wine	6 slices rough country bread, toasted

SAUTÉ THE ONION in a pan with the oil. Add the chicken livers, breaking them up as they cook. Add the wine and cook 2 to 3 minutes. Then add the capers and the tomato purée, diluted in a little chicken stock. Cook about 15 minutes, adding more stock if necessary. The mixture should have the consistency of thick cream. Serve hot on toasted bread. (For a smoother-textured pâté, the mixture can be blended in a food processor.)   SERVES 6

WHITE BEANS WITH GARLIC AND OIL

Fagioli all'Uccelletto

(Buca dell'Orafo)

1 pound cannellini beans
Olive oil
3 cloves garlic, chopped
Sage leaves
1 pound fresh tomatoes, peeled
  and chopped
Salt and pepper

SOAK THE BEANS overnight, then rinse and boil in salted water for 40 minutes, or until tender. In a separate pan, heat the oil and add the garlic, sage leaves, and pepper. Cook a few minutes, then add the drained beans. Add the tomatoes and salt and pepper, cover the pan, and cook about 15 minutes.   SERVES 4

WHITE BEANS WITH TUNA

Fagioli con Tonno

(Cave di Maiano)

1 pound dried white beans
¼ cup olive oil
2 cans imported oil-packed tuna
Pepper
½ onion, chopped
Fresh parsley

Soak the beans overnight, then boil in slightly salted water until tender but not overcooked. Drain well. Place the beans in a serving dish and drizzle with the oil. Drain the tuna and break it into chunks. Arrange in the dish over the beans. Season with pepper and sprinkle with the onion and parsley.   Serves 6

ONION SHELLS FILLED WITH ONION MAYONNAISE

(Principesa Elena Corsini)

In a large pot of salted boiling water, parboil some large white or yellow onions for about 5 to 10 minutes. Drain. Peel, and scoop out the centers, taking care to leave the shells intact. Chop the rest of the onions into very small pieces.

To make the mayonnaise put 3 large egg yolks into a bowl and, using a wooden spoon, beat them, slowly adding in 1½ to 2 cups olive oil, drop by drop. Continue stirring until all the oil has been incorporated and the mayonnaise is quite stiff. Mix some salt into about ½ tablespoon (or more according to taste) of lemon juice and slowly add to the mayonnaise. Next, bind the chopped onions with a small amount of mayonnaise. Fill the onion shells with the onion-mayonnaise mixture. Chill before serving.

TUSCAN FRITTERS

Fritto Toscano

(Marchesa Nerina Corsini Incisa della Rocchetta)

Stuff zucchini flowers with a soft cheese or anchovies. Combine some egg, flour, and salt to make a batter with a creamlike consistency. Dust the zucchini flowers in some flour, then dip in the batter and fry in hot oil. This process can also be used with artichokes (first score the base), onion rings, or green tomatoes. Serve with meat or poultry. Any leftovers can be put in a dish, covered with a tomato sauce, and baked in the oven.

ISMAIL'S EGG CURRY WITH BASIL

1 large red onion, peeled and chopped

Olive oil

8 cloves

4 large tomatoes

4 to 5 cloves garlic, peeled and minced

1 red chili pepper, chopped

¼ teaspoon salt

¼ teaspoon pepper

12 hard-boiled eggs, peeled and halved

Fresh basil leaves

Fry the chopped onion in olive oil. Add the cloves. Cut the tomatoes into chunks and add to the onions. Then add the garlic, chili pepper, salt and pepper. Cook 15 minutes over medium heat. Add the eggs to the tomato mixture. Cook another 5 minutes over low heat. Garnish with whole basil leaves.   SERVES 6 TO 8

FRITTATA WITH CHEESE

Frittata con Cacio

(VIRGINIA MARASCO)

4 tablespoons olive oil
8 slices pecorino cheese
8 eggs
Salt and pepper

IN A HEAVY OMELETTE pan heat the oil and cook the cheese slices just until they start to melt. Beat the eggs, season with salt and pepper. Raise the heat and pour the eggs over the cheese. When the eggs begin to set, lower the heat and cook the eggs through. Slide the frittata out of the pan and invert onto a plate; raise the heat and return the frittata to the pan for a couple of minutes to finish cooking.   SERVES 4

ISMAIL'S PESTO FRITTATA LACED WITH GREEN CHILIS

4 eggs
2 tablespoons milk
Salt
1½ tablespoons olive oil
1 green chili pepper, chopped
1 clove garlic, chopped
1 teaspoon pesto
Pinch of chili powder

BREAK THE EGGS into a bowl and beat well, then add the milk and a little salt. Heat the oil in a skillet and sauté the chili pepper and garlic. Add the pesto, mixing it well, and cook 3 to 4 minutes, stirring the ingredients all the time. Sprinkle with chili powder, then pour the eggs into the pan, but do not stir them. Cover with a lid and let the eggs cook 5 minutes over a medium heat. Remove the cover, flip the frittata into a half-moon shape, cover again, and leave a few more minutes. Serve with Italian bread or Indian *nan*.   SERVES 2

ZUCCHINI TORTE

Tortino di Zucchini

(Cave di Maiano)

4 zucchini
Olive oil
4 eggs
Grated Parmesan cheese
2 tablespoons fresh cream
Salt and pepper

Slice the zucchini and fry them in oil in a sauté pan. Beat the eggs with a little grated Parmesan and cream. Add the eggs to the zucchini and cook over a high heat for 2 minutes. Or, put the mixture on a hot iron plate and bake in a hot oven 5 to 7 minutes. Add salt and pepper before serving.   Serves 6

TOMATO TORTE

Tortino di Pomodori

(Virginia Marasco)

1 clove garlic, crushed
½ onion, finely chopped
½ hot chili pepper, chopped
Olive oil
4 ripe tomatoes, peeled,
  seeded, and chopped

6 basil leaves, shredded
6 eggs, beaten
Salt and pepper
Pecorino cheese, grated
Fresh country-style bread

Soften the garlic, onion, and chili pepper in oil over a low heat. Add the tomatoes and basil. Cover and cook until the tomatoes have turned to a pulp. Add the beaten eggs, salt and pepper. Continue to cook over a low heat. When the eggs are firm but still creamy on top, sprinkle with grated pecorino cheese and place under a hot broiler just until the cheese bubbles. Serve hot with crusty bread.   Serves 4

MIXED SEAFOOD ANTIPASTO

Antipasto di Mare

(Il Cavallino)

2 pounds clams
2 pounds mussels
Olive oil
Chopped fresh parsley
2 cloves garlic, chopped
Pepper
2 pounds cuttlefish
1 quart white vinegar
2 pounds prawns

FOR GARNISH:
Sweet peppers, diced
Chopped garlic
Chopped parsley
Olive Oil
Lemon juice

IN A 5-QUART POT steam the clams and the mussels with some olive oil, parsley, garlic, and pepper for about 10 minutes, or until the shells open. Remove from heat and set aside. Put the cuttlefish in a pot of boiling salted water and vinegar. Add the cork from a wine bottle and simmer for about 30 minutes; about 5 to 10 minutes before done, add the prawns. Drain the cuttlefish and prawns and leave to cool. To serve, cut the cuttlefish into pieces, put all the fish on a platter, and garnish with finely cut sweet peppers, garlic, parsley, olive oil, and lemon juice.   SERVES 8 TO 10

SOUP

LEEK AND TOMATO SOUP

Pappa al Pomodoro

(Cave di Maiano)

1 cup olive oil

1 leek, peeled and chopped

3 to 4 cloves garlic, crushed

1 pound fresh tomatoes, peeled
and chopped

Fresh basil leaves, shredded

1 pound day-old good country bread

Salt and pepper

Stock

*S*AUTÉ THE CHOPPED leek in the olive oil, then add the garlic. Add the tomatoes
and basil, bring to a boil, reduce heat, and simmer 5 to 10 minutes. Add the bread,
broken into small pieces, salt and pepper, and enough stock to make a thick consistency. The soup should not become too watery. Bring to a boil and cook about 2 to
3 minutes. Remove from heat and let soup rest for 30 minutes. Add olive oil when
serving. This soup has a coarse texture. For a smoother soup whip with a whisk.

SERVES 8

SPECIAL CORSINI SOUP

Carabaccia

(Contessa Lucrezia Corsini)

2 pounds onions, sliced
¼ cup olive oil
1 stalk celery, finely sliced
1½ quarts chicken stock
1 cup white wine

¼ pound green vegetables (peas,
   beans, etc.)
Parmesan cheese (or pecorino)
Sliced Italian bread (or toasted)

In a stockpot heat the olive oil and stir in the onions and celery. Sauté gently about 30 minutes. During this time, gradually add about 2 cups of the chicken stock. Then add the white wine, raise the heat, and when the wine has evaporated, add the green vegetables. Stir in the rest of the chicken stock. Lower the heat and cook until the vegetables are soft. Add grated Parmesan or pecorino cheese to the soup just before serving, if desired. To serve, put a slice of good bread in each bowl before adding the soup.   Serves 4

SOUP WITH PEPPERS

Acquacotta con Peperoni

(Virginia Marasco)

2 tablespoons olive oil
1 onion, chopped
2 cloves garlic, chopped
1 celery stalk, chopped
2 large sweet peppers, sliced

1 large tomato, peeled, seeded,
   and chopped
2 cups prepared stock
Salt and pepper
Sliced Italian bread, toasted and
   rubbed with garlic

Heat the olive oil in a large pot, and stir in the onion, garlic, and celery. Sauté gently without browning. Add the sweet peppers and cook over low heat until they soften. Then stir in the tomato and about ½ cup of the stock. Season with salt and pepper. Cook a few minutes, then add the remaining stock and simmer gently 20 to 30 minutes. To serve, put the toasted bread in soup bowls and pour the soup over the bread.   Serves 2 to 4

VEGETABLE SOUP

Zuppa di Verdura

(Coco Lezzone)

½ cup olive oil
1 large onion
2 tomatoes, peeled and broken into chunks
Fresh thyme, minced
2 carrots, chopped
2 stalks celery plus their leaves, chopped
2 large potatoes, peeled and cubed
4 cabbage leaves, chopped
1¼ cup cooked white cannellini beans
Small bunch fresh parsley
Salt and pepper

HEAT THE OLIVE OIL in a large stockpot. Add the onion and cook over a low heat until translucent. Stir in the tomatoes and thyme, and enough water to cover the vegetables by about 3 inches. Bring to a boil, lower heat, and simmer over a low heat about 45 minutes. Add the carrots and the celery. Cook 15 minutes. Then add the potatoes, cabbage, beans, parsley, and salt and pepper to taste. Simmer over a gentle heat until all the vegetables are tender. The soup should be very thick with only enough liquid to keep the vegetables suspended. If necessary, add a little more water when cooking.   SERVES 6

COLD MINESTRONE WITH RICE

Minestrone Freddo di Riso

(Coco Lezzone)

BEGIN WITH the recipe for Zuppa di Verdura. Then add some cooked rice and simmer together about 3 minutes. Let the soup cool, and serve.

RIBOLLITA

Ribollita

(COCO LEZZONE)

*Zuppa di Verdura (leftover Zuppa di
    Verdura is fine)*
Day-old Italian bread, sliced
Olive oil
1 can cannellini beans
Salt and pepper

POUR ENOUGH OIL to a depth of about ½ inch in a deep saucepan or stockpot and cover with a layer of the sliced bread. Gently pour some soup over the bread and season with a little salt, pepper, and olive oil. Add another layer of bread, then more soup, seasonings, and oil; continue layering until the pan is reasonably full. After adding the final layer of soup, sprinkle the cannellini beans over the top. Cook over a medium-low heat until the soup is thoroughly heated through.   SERVES 4

PORCINI MUSHROOM SOUP

Zuppa dei Funghi Porcini

(ELIZABETH MARANGONI)

*1 pound fresh porcini mushrooms
    (or other wild mushrooms)*
Olive oil
Salt and pepper
Fresh mint leaves

1 quart beef stock
1 to 2 cloves garlic, crushed
2 tablespoons chopped fresh parsley
Sliced Italian bread, toasted

THIS SOUP should be made with fresh porcini mushrooms, but as these are difficult to come by outside Italy, substitute any wild variety of mushrooms, but avoid cultivated mushrooms. Slice the mushrooms into small pieces and sauté in a deep saucepan with olive oil, salt and pepper, and a few mint leaves. When the mushrooms are browned add the beef stock and simmer about 15 minutes. Just before serving, stir in the garlic and parsley. Put the toasted bread in soup bowls. Ladle the soup over and serve hot.   SERVES 4

MARCHESA NERINA CORSINI
INCISA DELLA ROCCHETTA'S SOUP

*C*HOP SOME BACON into small pieces and fry until well cooked. In the same skillet, fry some chopped shallots, onions, and/or leeks until they become transparent, adding some oil if necessary. Add a packet of thawed frozen prepared soup vegetables (first removing the tomatoes and most of the carrots, if desired). Stir with the bacon and onions and cook gently until the mixture thickens. Add some chopped small potatoes, a small amount of boiling water, and a crust of Parmesan cheese. Cook about 25 minutes. Just before the end of cooking, add two sprigs of fresh marjoram or oregano. If the potatoes have not become cooked through by this time, break them up with a fork, which will also thicken the soup. Add half of a vegetable stock cube to the mixture if the soup needs further seasoning, but do not add salt.

This soup can be eaten hot or cold, and is particularly good poured over toasted bread soaked in olive oil. Vegetarians can dispense with the bacon—it is equally good without.

PASTA
AND RICE

PASTA WITH SWEET PEPPER SAUCE

(Virginia Marasco)

3 large red and yellow sweet peppers
Olive oil
1 cup cream
1½ pounds conchigli pasta

Cut the peppers into strips and put in a large saucepan with some olive oil and water. Cook on a very low heat for 1½ to 2 hours, until the mixture has thickened into a pulp and all the water has been absorbed. Add the cream and cook another 5 minutes, stirring all the time. Meanwhile, cook the conchigli (shell-shaped pasta), undercooking slightly. Then add it to the pan with the sauce and gently cook 2 minutes. Serve at once, but do not add cheese.   Serves 6 to 8

ROSANNA'S PENNE WITH TOMATOES

Rosanna's Penne Pomarolo

3½ pounds canned or fresh tomatoes
½ stalk celery, finely chopped
1 carrot, finely chopped
1 medium onion, finely chopped
2 tablespoons chopped fresh basil
1 teaspoon chopped fresh parsley
1 tablespoon olive oil
1½ pounds penne pasta
Parmesan cheese, grated

IN A SAUCEPAN cook the tomatoes, celery, carrot, onion, basil, parsley, and 1 tablespoon of olive oil 40 to 60 minutes, stirring occasionally. Five minutes before the end of cooking add a little more basil. If the sauce seems too dry, add a small amount of hot water; the consistency should be like thick cream. Combine with the cooked penne and serve with freshly grated Parmesan cheese.   SERVES 6

ISMAIL'S EXPLOSIVE PASTA SAUCE

3 red onions, peeled and chopped
8 cloves garlic, chopped
12 cloves
2 red chili peppers, sliced
15 tomatoes, peeled and chopped
Salt

Juice of 1 lemon
½ to 1 cup olive oil
2 handfuls fresh basil, roughly chopped
3 pounds penne pasta

IN A LARGE SAUCEPAN, cook the onions, garlic, cloves, chili peppers, tomatoes, salt, and lemon juice over a medium-high heat 15 minutes, stirring occasionally. Stir in the olive oil and basil, and cook a further 5 minutes. Cook the penne, drain, and combine well with the sauce before serving.   SERVES 16

FARFALLE WITH TUNA

Farfalle al Tonno

(Cave di Maiano)

3 tablespoons olive oil
2 cloves garlic, chopped
Fresh parsley, chopped
2 teaspoons Tabasco sauce
1 can imported oil-packed tuna
1¼ pounds canned peeled plum tomatoes
1 teaspoon dried oregano
1½ pounds farfalle pasta

*I*N A SKILLET HEAT the olive oil. Add the garlic, chopped parsley, and Tabasco and sauté 5 minutes. Stir in the tuna, tomatoes, and oregano. Cook 10 minutes. Cook the farfalle pasta, drain, and serve with the sauce. SERVES 6

FARFALLE WITH PEAS

Farfalle con Piselli

(Coco Lezzone)

2 spring onions, finely chopped
2 tablespoons olive oil
2½ pounds shelled fresh garden peas
¼ pound prosciutto (optional)
1 pound farfalle pasta

*S*AUTÉ THE SPRING onions in the olive oil until soft. Add the peas (if the peas are not very sweet add a pinch of sugar) and a little water. Cook about 10 minutes (or less if the peas are very small). Add salt and pepper, and the prosciutto, if desired. Cook the farfalle and drain. Toss with the sauce and serve. SERVES 4 TO 6

TAGLIARINI WITH WALNUT SAUCE

Tagliarini con Salsa di Noci

(Contessa Lucrezia Corsini)

1 cup walnuts

¼ cup pine nuts

2 tablespoons bread crumbs

2 cloves garlic

Fresh basil

½ cup milk

3 tablespoons olive oil

Salt and pepper

1 pound tagliarini pasta

In a blender or food processor container briefly spin the walnuts and pine nuts. Add the rest of the ingredients (except the pasta) and combine until the sauce has the consistency of thick cream—if it is too thick add a little more milk. Cook the tagliarini and drain. Toss with the sauce and sprinkle with coarsely chopped walnuts.

SERVES 4

TAGLIATELLE WITH FRESH PORCINI MUSHROOMS

Tagliatelle con Funghi Porcini

(Il Cavallino)

2 pounds onions, finely chopped

3 cloves garlic

1 stick butter

1 pound funghi porcini, finely diced

1 pint cream

Salt and pepper

1½ pounds tagliatelle pasta

Put the onions and garlic in a saucepan with the butter. Cook slowly until the onions are soft. Add the mushrooms and cook over medium heat about 30 minutes. Then stir in the cream and season with salt and pepper. Cook over medium heat about 10 minutes. Cook the tagliatelle, drain, and serve with the sauce.

SERVES 4 TO 6

ISMAIL'S VARIATION ON RICE AND BEANS

Ismail's Variation on Risi e Bisi

½ cup olive oil

2 tablespoons green pepper mustard

Lemon juice

2 cinnamon sticks

3 cups homemade chicken broth

3 cups patina rice

½ pound peas

Salt

2 fresh hot red chili peppers

1 teaspoon black mustard seeds

4 hard-boiled eggs, diced

IN A SAUCEPAN combine the olive oil, green pepper mustard, and some lemon juice, and cook a few minutes. Add the cinnamon sticks and cook about 5 minutes. Stir in the chicken broth plus 2 cups of water. Bring to a boil and add the rice, peas, and about ½ teaspoon salt. Add the chili peppers and mustard seeds. Cover and cook over a gentle heat, stirring frequently, until the rice is cooked. Just before serving, stir in the hard-boiled eggs. Serve hot.   SERVES 4

SALAD

ROSANNA'S TOMATO, MOZZARELLA, AND BASIL SALAD

Ripe tomatoes
Fresh mozzarella
Fresh basil
Extra-virgin olive oil
Salt

SLICE SOME LARGE ripe tomatoes and some mozzarella. In a serving dish arrange a slice of mozzarella over a slice of tomato, slightly overlapping, then top with one whole fresh basil leaf. Repeat with remaining slices. Generously drizzle with olive oil and sprinkle with salt.

ISMAIL'S CANNELLINI AND SWEET PEPPER SALAD

1 pound cooked cannellini beans
2 roasted red and yellow sweet peppers,
thinly sliced
1 head radicchio, shredded
Olive oil
Lemon juice
1 teaspoon cumin

DRAIN THE CANNELLINI beans and put in a serving bowl. Add the sweet peppers and radicchio. Dress with olive oil, lemon juice, and cumin.   SERVES 4

BROCCOLI SALAD

(CONTESSA LUCREZIA CORSINI)

2 bunches broccoli
4 small carrots
Olive oil
½ teaspoon hot red chili powder
Juice of 4 lemons
Salt
Black pepper

SOAK THE BROCCOLI in cold water 30 minutes. Cut the broccoli into strips about 2 inches long and ½ inch thick, and trim the florets. Bring some salted water to a boil and cook the broccoli stems 5 minutes. Then add the florets and cook a further 4 minutes. Meanwhile, peel and shred the carrots and put them into a bowl of ice water for 5 minutes. Mix the oil, chili powder, lemon juice, salt and pepper together. Drain the broccoli well and put into a bowl. Pour half the dressing over the broccoli and toss well. Drain the carrots, put them into a bowl and toss with the remaining dressing. Then add the carrots to the broccoli and mix well.   SERVES 6

ISMAIL'S SPINACH SALAD

1 pound fresh spinach
Olive oil
Vinegar
Salt and pepper
1 teaspoon black mustard seeds
3 cloves garlic, crushed

Wᴀꜱʜ, ᴄʟᴇᴀɴ, and thoroughly dry the spinach. Put in a serving bowl and toss with a basic dressing of olive oil, vinegar, salt and pepper, to which is added the black mustard seeds and crushed garlic.   Sᴇʀᴠᴇꜱ 3 ᴛᴏ 4

ISMAIL'S RADICCHIO
AND SPRING ONION SALAD

6 spring onions, sliced
2 heads radicchio
4 cloves garlic
½ teaspoon black pepper
Olive oil
Vinegar
Salt
2 tablespoons coarsely chopped walnuts

Pᴜᴛ ᴛʜᴇ ꜱᴘʀɪɴɢ onions in a bowl with the whole radicchio leaves. Crush the garlic with the black pepper, and add to a dressing of olive oil and wine vinegar. Season with salt to taste, and toss with the salad and coarsely chopped walnuts.   Sᴇʀᴠᴇꜱ 4

ISMAIL'S GREEN BEAN SALAD

1 pound green beans

6 cloves garlic

Olive oil

Lemon juice

Salt and pepper

1 teaspoon dried dill

STEAM THE green beans. Slice the garlic and add to a dressing of olive oil, lemon juice, salt, pepper, and dill. Pour over the beans. This salad can be served hot or cold.

SERVES 3 TO 4

ITALIAN BREAD SALAD

Panzanella

(MARCHESA NERINA CORSINI INCISA DELLA ROCCHETTA)

1 loaf day-old Italian bread

4 tomatoes

2 tablespoons finely chopped onion

2 tablespoons chopped cucumber

1 stalk celery, chopped

2 sweet peppers (red, yellow, or green), chopped

Fresh basil

Olive oil

Vinegar

Salt and pepper

BREAK UP THE bread into very small pieces (almost bread crumbs) and put in a dish. Take some extremely ripe tomatoes and cut into chunks over the bread. Add the onion, cucumber, celery, sweet peppers, fresh basil leaves, and combine well. Let the panzanella rest at room temperature 1 to 1½ hours (do not refrigerate). Before serving, season with olive oil, vinegar, and salt and pepper to taste.

This is the basic panzanella. To this can be added capers, tuna fish, hard-boiled eggs, anchovies, and also pepocino—a peppery type of rosemary.　SERVES 4 TO 6

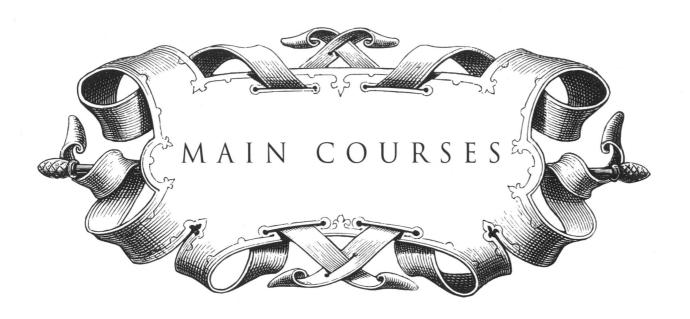

MAIN COURSES

ISMAIL'S FISH

4 medium firm-fleshed whole fish (in Italy
   I use mormore fish, which belong to the
   anchovy family)
Juice of 1 lemon
2 to 3 tablespoons mustard
4 sprigs fresh rosemary
6 cloves garlic, chopped
½ teaspoon salt
12 whole black peppercorns
5 large mushrooms
Olive oil

RINSE THE FISH, pat dry, and put in a pan. Mix the lemon juice with the mustard
and coat the fish. Pat the fish with the rosemary, garlic, salt, and peppercorns. Bake
in a preheated 350° oven 20 minutes, or until the fish is cooked through. Meanwhile
slice the mushrooms and sauté them in olive oil for 10 minutes. Garnish the fish with
the sautéed mushrooms and serve.   SERVES 4

TROUT WITH TOMATOES AND BASIL

Trote al Pomodor e Basilico

(CONTESSA LUCREZIA CORSINI)

4 fresh trout
4 tablespoons olive oil
2 cloves garlic, chopped
2 very large tomatoes, peeled, seeded,
  and pulped
Salt and pepper
Fresh basil leaves, shredded

CLEAN THE TROUT, rinse, and pat dry. Heat the oil in a sauté pan and cook the garlic until soft. Add the trout and turn them once in the oil. Add the fresh tomato pulp, spreading it around the trout, and season with salt and pepper and the basil. Cover and simmer over a low heat until the fish is cooked through.　　SERVES 4

ISMAIL'S FISH WITH PESTO

Ismail's Pesce con Pesto

1 whole fish (about 1½ pounds)
  —pomfret, salmon, bass, red or gray mullet
3 teaspoons pesto
2 tablespoons vinegar
2 cloves garlic, chopped
¼ cup olive oil
½ teaspoon black mustard seeds
Salt

WASH AND CLEAN the fish, and pat dry. Mix the pesto with the vinegar and garlic. Heat the oil in a pan, add the mustard seeds and cook 4 minutes on a medium heat. Coat the fish all over with the pesto mixture. Increase the heat and when the oil is very hot add the fish and sprinkle with a little salt. Reduce heat to medium, cover the pan, and cook 3 minutes. Turn the fish, cover again, and cook another 3 minutes.　　SERVES 2

ISMAIL'S FISH ROE WITH PESTO

½ pound fish roe

2 teaspoons pesto

¼ teaspoon chili powder

½ teaspoon cumin seeds

Juice of ½ lemon

2 tablespoons olive oil

2 cloves garlic, chopped

BOIL THE ROE in slightly salted water for 5 minutes, then drain. Mix the pesto with the chili powder, cumin seeds, and lemon juice. Put the oil in a pan and sauté the garlic until barely colored. Coat the roe with the pesto mixture and add to the pan. Cover and cook 3 minutes on a medium heat. Turn the roe and cook another 3 minutes. Serve hot.   SERVES 2

TRIPE FLORENTINE-STYLE

Trippa alla Fiorentina

(MIRO PINZAUTI'S TRIPE STALL)

LIGHTLY COOK ONIONS in olive oil until translucent. Slice the tripe into long strips and add to the onions. Add chopped tomatoes and stew ½ to ¾ of an hour, stirring from time to time. Turn off the heat. Add butter and Parmesan cheese, and serve with bread.

CHICKEN WITH PEPPERS

Pollo all'Arrabiata

(VIRGINIA MARASCO)

3 tablespoons olive oil
1 large onion, finely chopped
2 cloves garlic, crushed
1 chicken, about 2½ pounds, cut up
Salt and pepper
1 cup chianti
½ to 1 crushed hot chili pepper
5 tomatoes, peeled, seeded, and chopped

HEAT THE OLIVE OIL in a large heavy pan or casserole and sauté the onion and garlic. Add the chicken, season with the chili pepper, salt, and pepper, and brown on all sides. Add the wine, and cook over a low heat until the wine is reduced by half. Stir in the tomatoes and cook about 20 to 30 minutes, or until the chicken is tender.

SERVES 4

VEAL SCALLOPINE

Scallopine al Vitello

(BUCA DELL'ORAFO)

8 large veal scallops, about 1½ pounds
1 egg, beaten
2 cups fresh bread crumbs
Olive oil
Fresh tomato sauce

COMBINE THE EGG and bread crumbs. Pass the scallops through the mixture. Fry them lightly in olive oil in a large skillet. Add some tomato sauce and cook about 5 to 10 minutes, or until the sauce has thickened somewhat.

SERVES 4

VEAL STEW A LA MARASCO

Stufatino di Vitello

(VIRGINIA MARASCO)

Olive oil

2 cloves garlic, crushed

¼ chili pepper

1½ pounds lean veal, cubed

Flour

1 cup white wine

2 large ripe tomatoes, peeled, seeded, and chopped

Salt and pepper

Fresh parsley, chopped

IN A CASSEROLE dish brown the garlic and chili pepper in oil. Dust the veal with flour and brown it in the casserole. Add the wine, raise the heat, and cook until wine has evaporated. Add the tomatoes, salt and pepper. Cover and simmer gently about 1 hour, or until the meat is tender. Sprinkle generously with chopped parsley before serving.   SERVES 4 TO 6

ROAST LEG OF LAMB IL CAVALLINO-STYLE

Agnello alla Cavallino

(IL CAVALLINO)

1 leg of lamb, 6 to 7 pounds

Fresh rosemary

Fresh sage

3 cloves garlic, minced

Salt and pepper

Olive oil, about 1 tablespoon

Small potatoes, roasted

CUT THE LAMB lengthwise, along the bone. Remove any fat. Make a stuffing of the rosemary, sage, garlic, salt and pepper, and press it into the opening. Tie the meat with string and place in a dish with enough oil to cover the bottom of the dish. Cook in a preheated 425° oven 1 to 1¼ hours. Add more oil and water if necessary. Serve with small roasted potatoes.   SERVES 6 TO 8

ISMAIL'S LAMB CHOPS WITH PESTO

COVER THE LAMB chops with pesto and dust with very fine bread crumbs. Fry in olive oil, turning once.

Note: This may also be done with chicken breasts.

LAMB WITH BLACK OLIVES
Agnello con Olive Nere

(CONTESSA LUCREZIA CORSINI)

> ¼ cup olive oil
> 2 cloves garlic, crushed
> Fresh rosemary sprigs
> 2½ pounds stewing lamb, cut into chunks
> 1 cup dry white wine
> 2 fresh ripe tomatoes, peeled, seeded,
>   and chopped
> Salt and pepper
> Stock
> 30 large black olives

IN A LARGE SKILLET heat the olive oil, and add the garlic and 2 sprigs of fresh rosemary. Gently sauté, and when the garlic is barely golden add the cubed lamb and brown. Pour in the wine and when it has almost evaporated add the tomatoes and sprinkle with salt and pepper. Add enough stock to keep the meat from drying out, cover, and cook about 15 minutes over a low heat. Add the olives to the lamb. (Fresh olives should be boiled for a few minutes before using. Canned or bottled olives should be rinsed in water.) Cover and cook very slowly about 1½ hours, or until the meat is tender. Add more stock or water if necessary.   SERVES 4 TO 6

BEEF STEW WITH PINE NUTS

Stracotto

(ELIZABETH MARANGONI)

3 tablespoons olive oil

1 onion, chopped

½ hot chili pepper

1 carrot, chopped

⅓ cup pine nuts

⅓ cup blanched almonds, toasted

⅓ cup raisins

2 tablespoons chopped fresh parsley

2 cloves garlic

4 pounds boned beef rump, rolled
 and tied

2 cups homemade beef stock

½ bottle Chianti classico

Salt and pepper

Fresh parsley

IN A LARGE CASSEROLE heat the olive oil and cook the onion, chili pepper, and carrot until soft. Chop the nuts, raisins, parsley, and garlic, combine, and set aside. Make small slits in the meat and stuff with half the nut mixture. Brown the meat in some oil in a pan. Add the browned beef, stock, and wine to the casserole. Cover and simmer about 2½ hours, or until the meat is tender. About 15 minutes before the meat is done, add the rest of the nut mixture. When cooked, remove the meat and cut the string. Reduce the sauce and serve over the meat. Garnish with parsley. SERVES 6 TO 8

VEGETABLES

ZUCCHINI-ONION CASSEROLE

Scarpaccia

(Cave di Maiano)

1 pound small zucchini
  (with flowers if possible)
2 eggs
½ cup milk and water, mixed
4 tablespoons flour

3 large spring onions, finely chopped
4 tablespoons grated Parmesan cheese
½ clove garlic, crushed
Salt and pepper
Olive oil

FINELY CHOP the zucchini, sprinkle with salt, and leave to drain 15 minutes. Meanwhile, prepare a batter by beating together the eggs, milk and water, and flour. Rinse the zucchini and pat dry. Stir the zucchini, spring onions, Parmesan cheese, and garlic into the batter, season with salt and pepper, and pour into one large or two small greased baking pans. (The batter should not be more than ½ inch deep.) Drizzle oil over the top and bake in a preheated 425° oven about 30 minutes, or until the custard has set and is slightly brown on top. SERVES 6

ISMAIL'S ZUCCHINI

4 zucchini
4 tablespoons butter
25 whole peppercorns
4 pieces dried red chili pepper

*H*ALVE AND SLICE zucchini into ½-inch chunks. Heat the butter in a sauté pan. Add the zucchini, peppercorns, and chili pepper, and sauté 5 minutes. Serve hot.

SERVES 3 TO 4

ISMAIL'S EGGPLANT FRITTERS

*M*AKE A BATTER using chickpea flour instead of ordinary flour. Slice the eggplant into rounds and dip into the batter. Fry until golden, drain on paper towels, and serve hot.

BAKED EGGPLANT

Melanzane al Forno

(VIRGINIA MARASCO)

2 eggplants
Olive oil
4 cloves garlic, sliced
Salt and pepper

*S*LICE THE EGGPLANTS lengthwise into pieces about 1 inch thick. Smear 2 baking dishes with 1 tablespoon of olive oil each. Put the eggplant slices in a single layer in each dish, and insert two slivers of garlic into each piece. Add salt and pepper and sprinkle oil over the slices. Bake in a preheated 425° oven about 25 minutes.

SERVES 4

ISMAIL'S VARIATION ON EGGPLANT PARMESAN

Ismail's Variation on Melanzane Parmigiana

½ cup olive oil

1 medium onion, peeled and sliced

2 cinnamon sticks

4 cloves garlic, sliced or chopped

2 fresh whole red chili peppers

4 medium tomatoes, coarsely chopped

1 teaspoon red chili powder

½ teaspoon salt

2 tablespoons good wine vinegar

3 small eggplants, cubed without peeling

Parmesan cheese

*H*EAT THE OLIVE OIL in a skillet and sauté the onion. Add the cinnamon sticks and cook, stirring, 6 to 7 minutes. Add the garlic, whole red chilis, tomatoes, chili powder, salt, and wine vinegar, and stir to combine well. Add the eggplant, cover, and cook over medium heat between 20 and 40 minutes, or until the eggplant is cooked, stirring frequently to prevent sticking. Remove the cinnamon sticks before serving. Stir in some freshly grated Parmesan cheese.   SERVES 4

GRILLED PORCINI MUSHROOMS

Porcini alla Griglia

(BUCA DELL'ORAFO)

4 large or 8 small porcini mushrooms

4 large cloves garlic

Parsley

Salt and pepper

Olive oil

*C*LEAN THE PORCINI and trim the stalks. Peel the garlic and cut into slivers. Pierce the caps of the porcini with the garlic slivers, pushing them into the flesh. Chop the parsley and combine with a pinch of salt and some black pepper. Press the parsley seasoning mixture gently into the gills of the porcini. Set the mushroom caps in a dish and pour olive oil generously over each one. Leave for about 15 minutes, then grill the porcini, turning twice and adding more oil as they cook.   SERVES 4

CHANTERELLE MUSHROOMS A LA CORSINI

Guatelli in Umido

(Contessa Lucrezia Corsini)

18 ounces chanterelle mushrooms
6 tablespoons olive oil
2 cloves garlic, finely sliced
Salt and pepper
Chopped fresh parsley

With a damp cloth clean the mushrooms and split them in half lengthwise. Heat the olive oil in a sauté pan and gently cook the garlic. Add the mushrooms. When the mushrooms start to release some of their juices add a little salt and pepper and sprinkle with chopped parsley. Simmer gently until the mushrooms are tender.

Serves 4

ISMAIL'S POTATOES

1 large onion, peeled and sliced
4 tablespoons olive oil
5 pounds potatoes, peeled and chopped
6 cloves garlic, chopped
½ teaspoon salt
1 teaspoon ground cumin
1 red chili pepper, broken into four pieces
4 tomatoes, sliced
½ pound frozen peas

In a large skillet brown the sliced onion in the olive oil. Add the potatoes, garlic, salt, cumin, and chili pepper. Cook, stirring over high heat for 5 minutes. Reduce heat to low, stir in 1 cup of cold water, cover the pan, and cook 15 minutes. Add the tomatoes and cook another 10 minutes. Defrost and strain the peas, add to the potatoes, and cook 10 more minutes, or until the potatoes are tender. Serve hot.

Serves 8 to 10

ISMAIL'S PESTO POTATOES

6 potatoes
2 tablespoons olive oil
1 small onion, peeled and finely chopped
2 cloves garlic, chopped
2 teaspoons pesto
¼ teaspoon salt

PEEL AND BOIL the potatoes until they are tender but still firm. Drain and set aside. Heat the oil in a skillet and cook the onion and garlic about 4 to 5 minutes, or until golden. Stir in the pesto and mix well. Cut the potatoes into slices or chunks and add to the pan. Season with salt, then cook a further 4 to 5 minutes over medium heat.   SERVES 3 TO 4

SWISS CHARD AND SPINACH WITH PINE NUTS
Bietole e Spinaci con Pinoli

(VIRGINIA MARASCO)

1 pound fresh spinach, cleaned and washed
1 pound Swiss chard, cleaned and washed
3 tablespoons olive oil
1 clove garlic
1 tablespoon pine nuts
1 tablespoon raisins
Salt and pepper

IN SEPARATE PANS boil the spinach and Swiss chard in salted water just until cooked. Drain and squeeze out remaining water. Set aside. Heat the olive oil in a skillet. Add the garlic, pine nuts, and raisins, and gently cook. Chop the spinach and Swiss chard and combine with the mixture in the skillet. Cook several minutes, add salt and pepper, and serve hot.   SERVES 4

STUFFED SWISS CHARD

Gambi di Bietola Ripieni

(Elizabeth Marangoni)

1 cup flour
Nutmeg
½ teaspoon salt
1 tablespoon olive oil, plus more for deep frying
2 tablespoons white wine
4 pounds Swiss chard
2 slices bread, crusts trimmed
2 large hard-boiled eggs
2 generous tablespoons capers, finely chopped
Salt and pepper
3 large egg whites
Lemon wedges

*F*IRST PREPARE the batter. Combine the flour, nutmeg, and salt in a bowl. Begin stirring in the olive oil and wine, then slowly add ¾ cup water. Let the batter rest for 1 hour.

Cut the Swiss chard stems into pieces 3 to 4 inches long and put them in a bowl of cold water for 30 minutes. Bring a large pot of salted water to a boil. Add the Swiss chard and boil about 3 to 5 minutes. Drain, refresh under running water, and set aside. Break the bread into small pieces and put in a bowl. Stir in the yolks of the hard-boiled eggs, capers, salt and pepper, and mix well. Fill half the Swiss chard stems with the seasoned bread stuffing. Cover with the remainder of the stems, pressing down well.

Beat the egg whites and carefully fold into the batter. Heat some oil in a deep fryer. Dip the stuffed Swiss chard in the batter and fry on each side about 2 to 3 minutes, or until brown. Drain and serve with lemon wedges.   SERVES 4 TO 6

Note: This is the traditional way of preparing this dish. When I make it I use dried red chili powder instead of pepper in the stuffing, and I also add cumin seeds, which go very well with capers.

DESSERT

PEACHES IN WINE

PEEL SOME peaches and slice in half. Cover with lemon juice, wine, and sugar. Marinate 3 to 4 hours before serving.

STRAWBERRIES AND LEMON JUICE

WASH AND DRY strawberries, and slice. Sprinkle with lemon juice and sugar and marinate 1 hour before serving.

ISMAIL'S STRAWBERRIES IN WINE

WASH AND HULL strawberries. Put in a large bowl and cover completely with good dry red wine, to which a few cloves have been added.

RED BERRIES IN WINE

CHOOSE VARIOUS kinds of red berries. Put them in a bowl and cover with good dry red wine.

ZABAGLIONE

Zabaione

(MARCELLO DANIELLI)

FOR EACH SERVING allow 2 egg yolks, 1½ tablespoons superfine sugar, and a generous amount of dry Marsala. Put the egg yolks, sugar, and Marsala into the top of a double boiler and whisk until creamy and pale yellow. Set over hot water and continue beating well by hand until the mixture foams and begins to thicken. The Zabaglione should be served hot.

RED WINE SORBET

Sorbetto al Vino

(MARCELLO DANIELI)

¾ cup sugar
2 cups red wine
Fresh mint
½ pound raspberries

BOIL THE SUGAR and the red wine with some mint leaves until the sugar is dissolved. Remove from heat. Add the raspberries, which have been slightly crushed, and leave for about 1 hour. Remove the mint leaves and put the mixture into a blender and blend. Freeze the mixture about 3 hours, stirring frequently.

SERVES 4

GRAPE BREAD

Schiacciata con l'Uva

(Virginia Marasco)

Make or buy bread dough for 1 loaf and add to it a little olive oil. Knead for a few minutes. Roll out the dough to a thickness of about 1 inch. On top of the rolled out dough scatter 1 pound of whole fresh red grapes. Leave the dough to rise then sprinkle with sugar and about a dozen halved walnuts. Bake in a preheated 350° oven 30 minutes. This can also be made in layers—one layer of dough, one layer of grapes and nuts, another of dough, etc. This is usually eaten accompanied by a glass of vin santo.

Makes 1 loaf

CREAM AND RUM PUDDING

Panna Cotta

(Marcello Danieli)

1 cup confectioner's sugar
½ cup superfine sugar
1 pint heavy cream
¼ cup milk
1 tablespoon gelatine
1 cup rum

Combine both sugars with the cream in a pan and heat, stirring, until the sugar melts, making sure the cream does not come to a boil. Remove from the heat. Heat the milk, without boiling, and in it melt the gelatin. Slowly pour the milk into the cream. Stir in the rum. Melt some sugar until it has caramelized and line individual molds or ramekins with it. Pour the cream mixture into them, and refrigerate 2 hours.

Serves 4

TIRAMISU

(Marcello Danieli)

Kahlua liqueur (or Aikermes, an apricot liqueur)
Strong sweet cold espresso coffee
Savoiardi biscuits (or panettone)
3 egg yolks
3 tablespoons superfine sugar
½ pound mascarpone
Heavy cream
Grated bittersweet chocolate, for garnish

COMBINE THE LIQUEUR and coffee in a shallow bowl. Dip one side of the biscuits into the liquid. Place biscuits in one layer in a dish. Beat the egg yolks with the sugar until they are creamy and pale yellow. Add the mascarpone and enough heavy cream to loosen it. Mix well by hand. Gently spread the egg-and-cream batter over the layer of biscuits, and refrigerate. Garnish with good quality grated bittersweet chocolate.

Note: A combination of brandy and good drinking Marsala may be substituted for the Kahlua.   SERVES 4

TIRAMISU
(A VARIATION CALLED ZUPPA DEL DUCA)

(MARCELLO DANIELI)

2 egg yolks
6 tablespoons superfine sugar
6 tablespoons vin santo
½ pound mascarpone
1 cup strong espresso coffee
1 egg white
1 cup heavy cream, whipped and chilled
Savoiardi biscuits
2 cups vin santo

BEAT THE EGG YOLKS with the sugar in a bain-marie over medium heat until they are pale yellow, but do not allow to come to a boil. Stir in the vin santo and mix well. Remove from heat. In a separate bowl blend the mascarpone with the coffee. Beat the egg white. Combine the egg white and heavy cream. Gently fold the cooled beaten egg yolks into the cream. Dip one side of the biscuits in the vin santo and put enough to make one layer in a dish. Cover with alternating layers of the cream mixture and mascarpone mixture, finishing with the cream layer. Refrigerate 2 hours before serving. SERVES 4 TO 6

GRANDMOTHERS TART

Torta Di Nonna

(Contessa Lucrezia Corsini)

1 pint milk
2 egg yolks
¼ cup superfine sugar
2 tablespoons flour
Melted butter

FOR THE PASTRY:
1½ cups flour
⅓ cup superfine sugar
1½ teaspoons baking powder
1 egg plus 1 egg yolk
1 stick butter, chilled

FOR THE TOPPING:
Almonds
Pine nuts
Confectioner's sugar

Heat the milk just until it begins to boil. Remove from heat. Beat together the egg yolks and superfine sugar; then beat in the 2 tablespoons flour. Add 1 tablespoon of the hot milk to the mixture and blend well, then add the mixture to the milk and return to the heat, stirring until the mixture thickens. Brush the top with some melted butter and leave to cool.

Make the pastry by combining the flour, sugar, and baking powder. Stir in the egg and egg yolk; then quickly work in the butter. Cover, and refrigerate at least 30 minutes. Cut the dough in half and roll out thinly into two circles. Place the first circle into a greased 8-inch pie plate and leave ½ inch of pastry hanging over the edge. Pour the cream into the pastry and fold the pastry inward and brush with water. Roll out the second circle and place over the cream, trim pastry at the border and press down well. Toast some almonds and pine nuts and cut the almonds into slivers. Sprinkle over the pastry, and bake in a preheated 350° oven about 30 minutes until the top is brown. Serve cold, sprinkled generously with confectioner's sugar.

MAKES 1 TART